# MznLnx

*Missing Links Exam Preps*

Exam Prep for

## Marketing: An Introduction

### Armstrong, Kotler, 8th Edition

The MznLnx Exam Prep is your link from the texbook and lecture to your exams.
The MznLnx Exam Preps are unauthorized and comprehensive reviews of your textbooks.

All material provided by MznLnx and Rico Publications (c) 2010
Textbook publishers and textbook authors do not particpate in or contribute to these reviews.

# MznLnx

### Rico Publications

*Exam Prep for Marketing: An Introduction*
8th Edition
Armstrong, Kotler

*Publisher:* Raymond Houge
*Assistant Editor:* Michael Rouger
*Text and Cover Designer:* Lisa Buckner
*Marketing Manager:* Sara Swagger
*Project Manager, Editorial Production:* Jerry Emerson
*Art Director:* Vernon Lowerui

*Product Manager:* Dave Mason
*Editorial Assitant:* Rachel Guzmanji
*Pedagogy:* Debra Long
*Cover Image:* Jim Reed/Getty Images
*Text and Cover Printer:* City Printing, Inc.
*Compositor:* Media Mix, Inc.

(c) 2010 Rico Publications
ALL RIGHTS RESERVED. No part of this work covered by the copyright may be reproduced or used in any form or by an means--graphic, electronic, or mechanical, including photocopying, recording, taping, Web distribution, information storage, and retrieval systems, or in any other manner--without the written permission of the publisher.

Printed in the United States
ISBN:

For more information about our products, contact us at:
Dave.Mason@RicoPublications.com

For permission to use material from this text or product, submit a request online to:
Dave.Mason@RicoPublications.com

# Contents

**CHAPTER 1**
*Marketing: Managing Profitable Customer Relationships*   1

**CHAPTER 2**
*Company and Marketing Strategy: Partnering to Build Customer Relationships*   9

**CHAPTER 3**
*The Marketing Environment*   17

**CHAPTER 4**
*Managing Marketing Information*   25

**CHAPTER 5**
*Consumer and Business Buyer Behavior*   37

**CHAPTER 6**
*Segmentation, Targeting, and Positioning*   46

**CHAPTER 7**
*Product, Services, and Branding Strategy*   54

**CHAPTER 8**
*New-Product Development and Product Life-Cycle Strategies*   65

**CHAPTER 9**
*Pricing: Understanding and Capturing Customer Value*   68

**CHAPTER 10**
*Marketing Channels and Supply Chain Management*   79

**CHAPTER 11**
*Retailing and Wholesaling*   85

**CHAPTER 12**
*Communicating Customer Value: Advertising, Sales Promotion, and Public Relations*   91

**CHAPTER 13**
*Communicating Customer Value: Personal Selling and Direct Marketing*   100

**CHAPTER 14**
*Marketing In the Digital Age*   106

**CHAPTER 15**
*The Global Marketplace*   114

**CHAPTER 16**
*Marketing Ethics and Social Responsibility*   122

**ANSWER KEY**   129

# TO THE STUDENT

### COMPREHENSIVE

The *MznLnx* Exam Prep series is designed to help you pass your exams. Editors at MznLnx review your textbooks and then prepare these practice exams to help you master the textbook material. Unlike study guides, workbooks, and practice tests provided by the texbook publisher and textbook authors, *MznLnx* gives you **all** of the material in each chapter in exam form, not just samples, so you can be sure to nail your exam.

### MECHANICAL

The MznLnx Exam Prep series creates exams that will help you learn the subject matter as well as test you on your understanding. Each question is designed to help you master the concept. Just working through the exams, you gain an understanding of the subject--its a simple mechanical process that produces success.

### INTEGRATED STUDY GUIDE AND REVIEW

MznLnx is not just a set of exams designed to test you, its also a comprehensive review of the subject content. Each exam question is also a review of the concept, making sure that you will get the answer correct without having to go to other sources of material. You learn as you go! Its the easiest way to pass an exam.

### HUMOR

Studying can be tedious and dry. MznLnx's instructional design includes moderate humor within the exam questions on occassion, to break the tedium and revitalize the brain

*Chapter 1. Marketing: Managing Profitable Customer Relationships*  1

1. Procter is a surname, and may also refer to:

   - Bryan Waller Procter (pseud. Barry Cornwall), English poet
   - Goodwin Procter, American law firm
   - _____, consumer products multinational

   a. Developed country
   b. Procter ' Gamble
   c. Push
   d. Comparison-Shopping agent

2. _____ is defined by the American _____ Association as the activity, set of institutions, and processes for creating, communicating, delivering, and exchanging offerings that have value for customers, clients, partners, and society at large. The term developed from the original meaning which referred literally to going to market, as in shopping, or going to a market to sell goods or services.

   _____ practice tends to be seen as a creative industry, which includes advertising, distribution and selling.

   a. Business marketing
   b. Product naming
   c. Gatefold
   d. Marketing

3. The _____ is generally accepted as the use and specification of the four p's describing the strategic position of a product in the marketplace. One version of the origins of the _____ starts in 1948 when James Culliton said that a marketing decision should be a result of something similar to a recipe. This version continued in 1953 when Neil Borden, in his American Marketing Association presidential address, took the recipe idea one step further and coined the term 'Marketing-Mix'.
   a. 6-3-5 Brainwriting
   b. Marketing mix
   c. Power III
   d. 180SearchAssistant

4. In economics, _____ is the desire to own something and the ability to pay for it. The term _____ signifies the ability or the willingness to buy a particular commodity at a given point of time .

   a. Demand
   b. Discretionary spending
   c. Market dominance
   d. Market system

5. A _____ is the space, actual or metaphorical, in which a market operates. The term is also used in a trademark law context to denote the actual consumer environment, ie. the 'real world' in which products and services are provided and consumed.
   a. 180SearchAssistant
   b. Power III
   c. 6-3-5 Brainwriting
   d. Marketplace

6. A _____ is a collection of symbols, experiences and associations connected with a product, a service, a person or any other artifact or entity.

   _____s have become increasingly important components of culture and the economy, now being described as 'cultural accessories and personal philosophies'.

Some people distinguish the psychological aspect of a _____ from the experiential aspect.

a. Status brand
c. Lovemarks
b. Naming rights
d. Brand

7. _____ is a term used in marketing as well as the title of an important marketing paper written by Theodore Levitt. This paper was first published in 1960 in the Harvard Business Review; a journal of which he was an editor.

Some commentators have suggested that its publication marked the beginning of the modern marketing movement.

a. Market share
c. Blind taste test
b. Distributed presence
d. Marketing myopia

8. _____ is an advertisement in which a particular product specifically mentions a competitor by name for the express purpose of showing why the competitor is inferior to the product naming it.

This should not be confused with parody advertisements, where a fictional product is being advertised for the purpose of poking fun at the particular advertisement, nor should it be confused with the use of a coined brand name for the purpose of comparing the product without actually naming an actual competitor. ('Wikipedia tastes better and is less filling than the Encyclopedia Galactica.')

In the 1980s, during what has been referred to as the cola wars, soft-drink manufacturer Pepsi ran a series of advertisements where people, caught on hidden camera, in a blind taste test, chose Pepsi over rival Coca-Cola.

a. GL-70
c. Comparative advertising
b. Heavy-up
d. Cost per conversion

9. A personal and cultural _____ is a relative ethic _____, an assumption upon which implementation can be extrapolated. A _____ system is a set of consistent _____s and measures that is soo not true. A principle _____ is a foundation upon which other _____s and measures of integrity are based.

a. Customization
c. Dolly Dimples
b. Value
d. Private branding

10. In economics, _____' is the art or science of controlling economic demand to avoid a recession. In natural resources management and environmental policy more generally, it refers to policies to control consumer demand for environmentally sensitive or harmful goods such as water and energy. Within manufacturing firms the term is used to describe the activities of demand forecasting, planning and order fulfillment.

a. 6-3-5 Brainwriting
c. 180SearchAssistant
b. Power III
d. Demand management

## Chapter 1. Marketing: Managing Profitable Customer Relationships

11. A _____ is a subgroup of people or organizations sharing one or more characteristics that cause them to have similar product and/or service needs. A true _____ meets all of the following criteria: it is distinct from other segments (different segments have different needs), it is homogeneous within the segment (exhibits common needs); it responds similarly to a market stimulus, and it can be reached by a market intervention. The term is also used when consumers with identical product and/or service needs are divided up into groups so they can be charged different amounts.

   a. Vertical market
   b. Market segment
   c. Societal marketing
   d. Law of disruption

12. _____ is a business discipline which is focused on the practical application of marketing techniques and the management of a firm's marketing resources and activities. Marketing managers are often responsible for influencing the level, timing, and composition of customer demand accepted definition of the term. In part, this is because the role of a marketing manager can vary significantly based on a business' size, corporate culture, and industry context.

   a. Fast moving consumer goods
   b. Performance-based advertising
   c. Door-to-door
   d. Marketing management

13. A _____ is a process that can allow an organization to concentrate its limited resources on the greatest opportunities to increase sales and achieve a sustainable competitive advantage. A _____ should be centered around the key concept that customer satisfaction is the main goal.

   A _____ is most effective when it is an integral component of corporate strategy, defining how the organization will successfully engage customers, prospects, and competitors in the market arena.

   a. Marketing strategy
   b. Vertical market
   c. Marketspace
   d. Law of disruption

14. In the field of marketing, a customer _____ consists of the sum total of benefits which a vendor promises that a customer will receive in return for the customer's associated payment (or other value-transfer.)

   Put simply, the _____ is what the customer gets for his money.

   Accordingly, a customer can evaluate a company's value-proposition on two broad dimensions with multiple subsets:

   1. relative performance: what the customer gets from the vendor relative to a competitor's offering;
   2. price: which consists of the payment the customer makes to acquire the product or service; plus the access cost

   The vendor-company's marketing and sales efforts offer a customer _____; the vendor-company's delivery and customer-service processes then fulfill that value-proposition.

   A value-proposition can assist in a firm's marketing strategy, and may guide a business to target a particular market segment.

**4**     *Chapter 1. Marketing: Managing Profitable Customer Relationships*

a. Market environment
c. Value proposition

b. Product differentiation
d. Law of disruption

15. In environmental modeling and especially in hydrology, a _____ model means a model that is acceptably consistent with observed natural processes, i.e. that simulates well, for example, observed river discharge. It is a key concept of the so-called Generalized Likelihood Uncertainty Estimation (GLUE) methodology to quantify how uncertain environmental predictions are.

a. Power III
c. 180SearchAssistant

b. 6-3-5 Brainwriting
d. Behavioral

16. A _____ is a plan of action designed to achieve a particular goal.

_____ is different from tactics. In military terms, tactics is concerned with the conduct of an engagement while _____ is concerned with how different engagements are linked.

a. Power III
c. 180SearchAssistant

b. 6-3-5 Brainwriting
d. Strategy

17. In economic models, the _____ time frame assumes no fixed factors of production. Firms can enter or leave the marketplace, and the cost (and availability) of land, labor, raw materials, and capital goods can be assumed to vary. In contrast, in the short-run time frame, certain factors are assumed to be fixed, because there is not sufficient time for them to change.

a. 180SearchAssistant
c. Power III

b. 6-3-5 Brainwriting
d. Long-run

18. _____ involves disseminating information about a product, product line, brand, or company. It is one of the four key aspects of the marketing mix. (The other three elements are product marketing, pricing, and distribution). P>_____ is generally sub-divided into two parts:

- Above the line _____: Promotion in the media (e.g. TV, radio, newspapers, Internet and Mobile Phones) in which the advertiser pays an advertising agency to place the ad
- Below the line _____: All other _____. Much of this is intended to be subtle enough for the consumer to be unaware that _____ is taking place. E.g. sponsorship, product placement, endorsements, sales _____, merchandising, direct mail, personal selling, public relations, trade shows

a. M80
c. Technology maturity lifecycle

b. Cash and carry
d. Promotion

19. The _____ concept is an enlightened marketing concept that holds that a company should make good marketing decisions by considering consumers' wants, the company's requirements, and society's long-term interests. It is closely linked with the principles of corporate social responsibility and of sustainable development.

The concept has an emphasis on social responsibility and suggests that for a company to only focus on exchange relationship with customers might not be suitable in order to sustain long term success.

*Chapter 1. Marketing: Managing Profitable Customer Relationships* 5

a. Societal marketing
b. Product differentiation
c. Customer acquisition management
d. Category management

20. _____ consists of the processes a company uses to track and organize its contacts with its current and prospective customers. _____ software is used to support these processes; information about customers and customer interactions can be entered, stored and accessed by employees in different company departments. Typical _____ goals are to improve services provided to customers, and to use customer contact information for targeted marketing.
a. Customer franchise
b. Social marketing
c. Buy one, get one free
d. Customer relationship management

21. _____, a business term, is a measure of how products and services supplied by a company meet or surpass customer expectation. It is seen as a key performance indicator within business and is part of the four perspectives of a Balanced Scorecard.

In a competitive marketplace where businesses compete for customers, _____ is seen as a key differentiator and increasingly has become a key element of business strategy.

a. Safety stock
b. Psychological pricing
c. Customer satisfaction
d. Street date

22. Customer _____ consists of the processes a company uses to track and organize its contacts with its current and prospective customers. CRelationship management software is used to support these processes; information about customers and customer interactions can be entered, stored and accessed by employees in different company departments. Typical CRelationship management goals are to improve services provided to customers, and to use customer contact information for targeted marketing.
a. Pinstorm
b. Kano model
c. Corporate image
d. Relationship management

23. A _____ is a type of business entity in which partners (owners) share with each other the profits or losses of the business undertaking in which all have invested. _____s are often favored over corporations for taxation purposes, as the _____ structure does not generally incur a tax on profits before it is distributed to the partners (i.e. there is no dividend tax levied.) However, depending on the _____ structure and the jurisdiction in which it operates, owners of a _____ may be exposed to greater personal liability than they would as shareholders of a corporation.
a. Colour trademark
b. Partnership
c. Contributory negligence
d. Screener

24. _____ is a market coverage strategy in which a firm decides to ignore market segment differences and go after the whole market with one offer.it is type of marketing (or attempting to sell through persuasion) of a product to a wide audience. The idea is to broadcast a message that will reach the largest number of people possible. Traditionally _____ has focused on radio, television and newspapers as the medium used to reach this broad audience.
a. Business-to-consumer
b. Product naming
c. Value chain
d. Mass marketing

## Chapter 1. Marketing: Managing Profitable Customer Relationships

25. _____ is a sub-discipline and type of marketing. There are two main definitional characteristics which distinguish it from other types of marketing. The first is that it attempts to send its messages directly to consumers, without the use of intervening media.
   a. Direct Marketing Associations
   b. Power III
   c. Database marketing
   d. Direct marketing

26. _____ is one of the four elements of marketing mix. An organization or set of organizations (go-betweens) involved in the process of making a product or service available for use or consumption by a consumer or business user.

The other three parts of the marketing mix are product, pricing, and promotion.

   a. Distribution
   b. LIFO
   c. Better Living Through Chemistry
   d. Clustering

27. A _____ or logistics network is the system of organizations, people, technology, activities, information and resources involved in moving a product or service from supplier to customer. _____ activities transform natural resources, raw materials and components into a finished product that is delivered to the end customer. In sophisticated _____ systems, used products may re-enter the _____ at any point where residual value is recyclable.
   a. Supply chain
   b. Wholesale
   c. Megalister
   d. Supply chain network

28. In marketing, customer _____, lifetime customer value (LCV), or _____ (LTV) and a new concept of 'customer life cycle management' is the present value of the future cash flows attributed to the customer relationship. Use of customer _____ as a marketing metric tends to place greater emphasis on customer service and long-term customer satisfaction, rather than on maximizing short-term sales.

Customer _____ has intuitive appeal as a marketing concept, because in theory it represents exactly how much each customer is worth in monetary terms, and therefore exactly how much a marketing department should be willing to spend to acquire each customer.

   a. Cannibalization
   b. Commercial planning
   c. Lifetime value
   d. Marketing strategy

29. The loyalty business model is a business model used in strategic management in which company resources are employed so as to increase the loyalty of customers and other stakeholders in the expectation that corporate objectives will be met or surpassed. A typical example of this type of model is: quality of product or service leads to customer satisfaction, which leads to _____, which leads to profitability.

Fredrick Reichheld (1996) expanded the loyalty business model beyond customers and employees.

   a. Customer loyalty
   b. Power III
   c. 6-3-5 Brainwriting
   d. 180SearchAssistant

30.

## Chapter 1. Marketing: Managing Profitable Customer Relationships

The net present value (NPV) of all of a company's customers in terms of customer loyalty and indirectly, the revenue that the company can obtain from them.

In deciding the value of a company, it is important to know of how much value its customer base is in terms of future revenues. The greater the _____ , the more future revenue in the lifetime of its clients; this means that a company with a higher _____ can get more money from its customers on average than another company that is identical in all other characteristics.

a. Hoarding
c. Household production function
b. Marginal revenue
d. Customer equity

31. _____, also referred to as i-marketing, web marketing, online marketing is the marketing of products or services over the Internet.

The Internet has brought many unique benefits to marketing, one of which being lower costs for the distribution of information and media to a global audience. The interactive nature of _____, both in terms of providing instant response and eliciting responses, is a unique quality of the medium.

a. Internet marketing
c. AMAX
b. ADTECH
d. ACNielsen

32. _____ is a term commonly used to describe commerce transactions between businesses like the one between a manufacturer and a wholesaler or a wholesaler and a retailer i.e both the buyer and the seller are business entity. This is unlike business-to-consumers (B2C) which involve a business entity and end consumer, or business-to-government (B2G) which involve a business entity and government.

The volume of B2B transactions is much higher than the volume of B2C transactions. The primary reason for this is that in a typical supply chain there will be many B2B transactions involving subcomponent or raw materials, and only one B2C transaction, specifically sale of the finished product to the end customer.

a. Disruptive technology
c. Customer analytics
b. Cannibalization
d. Business-to-business

33. Electronic commerce, commonly known as _____ or eCommerce, consists of the buying and selling of products or services over electronic systems such as the Internet and other computer networks. The amount of trade conducted electronically has grown extraordinarily with wide-spread Internet usage. A wide variety of commerce is conducted in this way, spurring and drawing on innovations in electronic funds transfer, supply chain management, Internet marketing, online transaction processing, electronic data interchange (EDI), inventory management systems, and automated data collection systems.

a. ADTECH
c. ACNielsen
b. AMAX
d. E-commerce

34. _____ in its literal sense is the process of transformation of local or regional phenomena into global ones. It can be described as a process by which the people of the world are unified into a single society and function together.

This process is a combination of economic, technological, sociocultural and political forces.

a. 180SearchAssistant  
b. Power III  
c. 6-3-5 Brainwriting  
d. Globalization

35. _____ is a branch of philosophy which seeks to address questions about morality, such as how a moral outcome can be achieved in a specific situation (applied _____), how moral values should be determined (normative _____), what moral values people actually abide by (descriptive _____), what the fundamental semantic, ontological, and epistemic nature of _____ or morality is (meta-_____), and how moral capacity or moral agency develops and what its nature is (moral psychology.)

Socrates was one of the first Greek philosophers to encourage both scholars and the common citizen to turn their attention from the outside world to the condition of man. In this view, Knowledge having a bearing on human life was placed highest, all other knowledge being secondary.

a. ADTECH  
b. ACNielsen  
c. AMAX  
d. Ethics

36. _____ is the systematic application of marketing along with other concepts and techniques to achieve specific behavioral goals for a social good. _____ can be applied to promote, for example, merit goods, make the society avoid demerit goods and thus to promote that considers society's well being as a whole. This may include asking people not to smoke in public areas, for example, ask them to use seat belts, prompting to make them follow speed limits.

a. Blind taste test  
b. Corporate image  
c. Social marketing  
d. Corporate capabilities package

## Chapter 2. Company and Marketing Strategy: Partnering to Build Customer Relationships

1. _____ is an organization's process of defining its strategy and making decisions on allocating its resources to pursue this strategy, including its capital and people. Various business analysis techniques can be used in _____, including SWOT analysis (Strengths, Weaknesses, Opportunities, and Threats ) and PEST analysis (Political, Economic, Social, and Technological analysis) or STEER analysis involving Socio-cultural, Technological, Economic, Ecological, and Regulatory factors and EPISTEL (Environment, Political, Informatic, Social, Technological, Economic and Legal)

_____ is the formal consideration of an organization's future course. All _____ deals with at least one of three key questions:

1. 'What do we do?'
2. 'For whom do we do it?'
3. 'How do we excel?'

In business _____, the third question is better phrased 'How can we beat or avoid competition?'. (Bradford and Duncan, page 1.)

a. 6-3-5 Brainwriting  
c. Power III  
b. Strategic planning  
d. 180SearchAssistant

2. _____ in organizations and public policy is both the organizational process of creating and maintaining a plan; and the psychological process of thinking about the activities required to create a desired goal on some scale. As such, it is a fundamental property of intelligent behavior. This thought process is essential to the creation and refinement of a plan, or integration of it with other plans, that is, it combines forecasting of developments with the preparation of scenarios of how to react to them.

a. 180SearchAssistant  
c. 6-3-5 Brainwriting  
b. Planning  
d. Power III

3. A _____ is a brief statement of the purpose of a company, organization. It is ideally used to guide the actions of the organization.

_____s often contain the following:

- Purpose of the organization
- The organization's primary stakeholders: clients, stockholders, etc.
- Responsibilities of the organization towards these stockholders
- Products and services offered

Generally shorter _____s are more effective than longer ones.

In developing a _____:

- Encourage input as feasible from employees, volunteers, and other stakeholders
- Publicize it broadly

The _____ can be used to resolve differences between business stakeholders. Stakeholders include: employees including managers and executives, stockholders, board of directors, customers, suppliers, distributors, creditors, governments (local, state, federal, etc.), unions, competitors, NGO's, and the general public.

a. Mission statement
b. Power III
c. 180SearchAssistant
d. 6-3-5 Brainwriting

4. The _____ is a marketing term and refers to all of the forces outside of marketing that affect marketing management's ability to build and maintain successful relationships with target customers. The _____ consists of both the macroenvironment and the microenvironment.

The microenvironment refers to the forces that are close to the company and affect its ability to serve its customers.

a. Market environment
b. Brochure
c. Vertical market
d. Marketing performance measurement and management

5. The _____ is a chart that had been created by Bruce Henderson for the Boston Consulting Group in 1970 to help corporations with analyzing their business units or product lines. This helps the company allocate resources and is used as an analytical tool in brand marketing, product management, strategic management, and portfolio analysis.

a. Sampling
b. AStore
c. Richard Buckminster 'Bucky' Fuller
d. BCG matrix

6. Radio-frequency identification (_____) is the use of an object (typically referred to as an _____ tag) applied to or incorporated into a product, animal, or person for the purpose of identification and tracking using radio waves. Some tags can be read from several meters away and beyond the line of sight of the reader.

Most _____ tags contain at least two parts.

a. 180SearchAssistant
b. 6-3-5 Brainwriting
c. Power III
d. RFID

7. _____ is understood as a business unit within the overall corporate identity which is distinguishable from other business because it serves a defined external market where management can conduct strategic planning in relation to products and markets. When companies become really large, they are best thought of as being composed of a number of businesses (or _____ s.)

In the broader domain of strategic management, the phrase '_____' came into use in the 1960s, largely as a result of General Electric's many units.

a. Strategic business unit
b. Cost leadership
c. Business strategy
d. Chaotics

## Chapter 2. Company and Marketing Strategy: Partnering to Build Customer Relationships

8. _____, in strategic management and marketing, is the percentage or proportion of the total available market or market segment that is being serviced by a company. It can be expressed as a company's sales revenue (from that market) divided by the total sales revenue available in that market. It can also be expressed as a company's unit sales volume (in a market) divided by the total volume of units sold in that market.
   a. Buy one, get one free
   b. Google Advertising Professional
   c. Market share
   d. Marketing strategy

9. In business, a _____ is a product or a business unit that generates unusually high profit margins: so high that it is responsible for a large amount of a company's operating profit. This profit far exceeds the amount necessary to maintain the _____ business, and the excess is used by the business for other purposes.

   A firm is said to be acting as a _____ when its earnings per share (EPS) is equal to its dividends per share (DPS), or in other words, when a firm pays out 100% of its free cash flow (FCF) to its shareholders as dividends at the end of each accounting term.

   a. Crisis management
   b. Voice of the customer
   c. Performance measurement
   d. Cash cow

10. _____ is a sub-discipline and type of marketing. There are two main definitional characteristics which distinguish it from other types of marketing. The first is that it attempts to send its messages directly to consumers, without the use of intervening media.
    a. Direct Marketing Associations
    b. Database marketing
    c. Power III
    d. Direct Marketing

11. _____ is defined by the American _____ Association as the activity, set of institutions, and processes for creating, communicating, delivering, and exchanging offerings that have value for customers, clients, partners, and society at large. The term developed from the original meaning which referred literally to going to market, as in shopping, or going to a market to sell goods or services.

    _____ practice tends to be seen as a creative industry, which includes advertising, distribution and selling.

    a. Business marketing
    b. Product naming
    c. Gatefold
    d. Marketing

12. _____ or _____ data refers to selected population characteristics as used in government, marketing or opinion research, or the _____ profiles used in such research. Note the distinction from the term 'demography' Commonly-used _____ include race, age, income, disabilities, mobility (in terms of travel time to work or number of vehicles available), educational attainment, home ownership, employment status, and even location.
    a. Albert Einstein
    b. AStore
    c. Demographic
    d. African Americans

13. A _____ strategy targets non-buying customers in currently targeted segments. It also targets new customers in new segments. (Winer)

## Chapter 2. Company and Marketing Strategy: Partnering to Build Customer Relationships

A marketing manager has to think about the following questions before implementing a _____ strategy: Is it profitable? Will it require the introduction of new or modified products? Is the customer and channel well enough researched and understood?

The marketing manager uses these four groups to give more focus to the market segment decision: existing customers, competitor customers, non-buying in current segments, new segments.

a. Pinstorm
b. Kano model
c. Market development
d. Business-to-business

14. _____ is one of the four growth strategies of the Product-Market Growth Matrix defined by Ansoff. _____ occurs when a company enters/penetrates a market with current products. The best way to achieve this is by gaining competitors' customers (part of their market share.)
a. Contestable market
b. Horizontal market
c. Market penetration
d. Competitive equilibrium

15. In business and engineering, new _____ is the term used to describe the complete process of bringing a new product or service to market. There are two parallel paths involved in the Nproduct development process: one involves the idea generation, product design, and detail engineering; the other involves market research and marketing analysis. Companies typically see new _____ as the first stage in generating and commercializing new products within the overall strategic process of product life cycle management used to maintain or grow their market share.
a. New product screening
b. New product development
c. Product optimization
d. Product development

16. A _____ or subscription radio is a digital radio signal that is broadcast by a communications satellite, which covers a much wider geographical range than terrestrial radio signals.

For now, _____ offers a meaningful alternative to ground-based radio services in some countries, notably the United States. Mobile services, such as Sirius, XM, and Worldspace, allow listeners to roam across an entire continent, listening to the same audio programming anywhere they go.

a. Power III
b. 6-3-5 Brainwriting
c. 180SearchAssistant
d. Satellite Radio

17. A personal and cultural _____ is a relative ethic _____, an assumption upon which implementation can be extrapolated. A _____ system is a set of consistent _____s and measures that is soo not true. A principle _____ is a foundation upon which other _____s and measures of integrity are based.
a. Private branding
b. Customization
c. Value
d. Dolly Dimples

18. The _____ is a concept from business management that was first described and popularized by Michael Porter in his 1985 best-seller, Competitive Advantage: Creating and Sustaining Superior Performance.

A _____ is a chain of activities. Products pass through all activities of the chain in order and at each activity the product gains some value.

## Chapter 2. Company and Marketing Strategy: Partnering to Build Customer Relationships 13

a. Blind taste test
b. Value chain
c. Distributed presence
d. Marketspace

19. The _____ is generally accepted as the use and specification of the four p's describing the strategic position of a product in the marketplace. One version of the origins of the _____ starts in 1948 when James Culliton said that a marketing decision should be a result of something similar to a recipe. This version continued in 1953 when Neil Borden, in his American Marketing Association presidential address, took the recipe idea one step further and coined the term 'Marketing-Mix'.

a. Power III
b. 6-3-5 Brainwriting
c. 180SearchAssistant
d. Marketing mix

20. A _____ is a process that can allow an organization to concentrate its limited resources on the greatest opportunities to increase sales and achieve a sustainable competitive advantage. A _____ should be centered around the key concept that customer satisfaction is the main goal.

A _____ is most effective when it is an integral component of corporate strategy, defining how the organization will successfully engage customers, prospects, and competitors in the market arena.

a. Law of disruption
b. Marketspace
c. Marketing strategy
d. Vertical market

21. A _____ is a plan of action designed to achieve a particular goal.

_____ is different from tactics. In military terms, tactics is concerned with the conduct of an engagement while _____ is concerned with how different engagements are linked.

a. Strategy
b. Power III
c. 6-3-5 Brainwriting
d. 180SearchAssistant

22. A _____ is a subgroup of people or organizations sharing one or more characteristics that cause them to have similar product and/or service needs. A true _____ meets all of the following criteria: it is distinct from other segments (different segments have different needs), it is homogeneous within the segment (exhibits common needs); it responds similarly to a market stimulus, and it can be reached by a market intervention. The term is also used when consumers with identical product and/or service needs are divided up into groups so they can be charged different amounts.

a. Market segment
b. Vertical market
c. Law of disruption
d. Societal marketing

23. In environmental modeling and especially in hydrology, a _____ model means a model that is acceptably consistent with observed natural processes, i.e. that simulates well, for example, observed river discharge. It is a key concept of the so-called Generalized Likelihood Uncertainty Estimation (GLUE) methodology to quantify how uncertain environmental predictions are.

a. 180SearchAssistant
b. Power III
c. 6-3-5 Brainwriting
d. Behavioral

## Chapter 2. Company and Marketing Strategy: Partnering to Build Customer Relationships

24. In marketing, _____ has come to mean the process by which marketers try to create an image or identity in the minds of their target market for its product, brand, or organization. It is the 'relative competitive comparison' their product occupies in a given market as perceived by the target market.

Re-_____ involves changing the identity of a product, relative to the identity of competing products, in the collective minds of the target market.

a. LIFO
b. Sigg bottles
c. Positioning
d. Per-inquiry advertising

25. _____ in economics and business is the result of an exchange and from that trade we assign a numerical monetary value to a good, service or asset. If I trade 4 apples for an orange, the _____ of an orange is 4 - apples. Inversely, the _____ of an apple is 1/4 oranges.

a. Price war
b. Price
c. Contribution margin-based pricing
d. Transfer pricing

26. _____ involves disseminating information about a product, product line, brand, or company. It is one of the four key aspects of the marketing mix. (The other three elements are product marketing, pricing, and distribution). P>_____ is generally sub-divided into two parts:

- Above the line _____: Promotion in the media (e.g. TV, radio, newspapers, Internet and Mobile Phones) in which the advertiser pays an advertising agency to place the ad
- Below the line _____: All other _____. Much of this is intended to be subtle enough for the consumer to be unaware that _____ is taking place. E.g. sponsorship, product placement, endorsements, sales _____, merchandising, direct mail, personal selling, public relations, trade shows

a. Technology maturity lifecycle
b. Promotion
c. M80
d. Cash and carry

27. _____ is an advertisement in which a particular product specifically mentions a competitor by name for the express purpose of showing why the competitor is inferior to the product naming it.

This should not be confused with parody advertisements, where a fictional product is being advertised for the purpose of poking fun at the particular advertisement, nor should it be confused with the use of a coined brand name for the purpose of comparing the product without actually naming an actual competitor. ('Wikipedia tastes better and is less filling than the Encyclopedia Galactica.')

In the 1980s, during what has been referred to as the cola wars, soft-drink manufacturer Pepsi ran a series of advertisements where people, caught on hidden camera, in a blind taste test, chose Pepsi over rival Coca-Cola.

a. Cost per conversion
b. GL-70
c. Heavy-up
d. Comparative advertising

## Chapter 2. Company and Marketing Strategy: Partnering to Build Customer Relationships

28. _____ is a strategic planning method used to evaluate the Strengths, Weaknesses, Opportunities, and Threats involved in a project or in a business venture. It involves specifying the objective of the business venture or project and identifying the internal and external factors that are favorable and unfavorable to achieving that objective. The technique is credited to Albert Humphrey, who led a research project at Stanford University in the 1960s and 1970s using data from Fortune 500 companies.

   a. Bitcom
   b. Corporate capabilities package
   c. Societal marketing
   d. SWOT analysis

29. _____ generally refers to a list of all planned expenses and revenues. It is a plan for saving and spending. A _____ is an important concept in microeconomics, which uses a _____ line to illustrate the trade-offs between two or more goods.

   a. 180SearchAssistant
   b. 6-3-5 Brainwriting
   c. Power III
   d. Budget

30. _____ is the realization of an application idea, model, design, specification, standard, algorithm an _____ is a realization of a technical specification or algorithm as a program, software component, or other computer system. Many _____s may exist for a given specification or standard.

   a. ADTECH
   b. ACNielsen
   c. AMAX
   d. Implementation

31. _____ is a corporate title referring to an executive responsible for various marketing in an organization. Most often the position reports to the chief executive officer.

   With primary or shared responsibility for areas such as sales management, product development, distribution channel management, public relations, marketing communications (including advertising and promotions), pricing, market research, and customer service.

   a. Tyco International
   b. Sustainable Forestry Initiative
   c. Chief marketing officer
   d. Point of sale

32. Procter is a surname, and may also refer to:

   - Bryan Waller Procter (pseud. Barry Cornwall), English poet
   - Goodwin Procter, American law firm
   - _____, consumer products multinational

   a. Comparison-Shopping agent
   b. Push
   c. Procter ' Gamble
   d. Developed country

33. _____ is an organizational lifecycle function within a company dealing with the planning or marketing of a product or products at all stages of the product lifecycle.

   _____ and product marketing (outbound focused) are different yet complementary efforts with the objective of maximizing sales revenues, market share, and profit margins. The role of _____ spans many activities from strategic to tactical and varies based on the organizational structure of the company.

a. Promise Index
b. Product management
c. Product catalogue management
d. Product information management

34. _____ is the practice of individuals including commercial businesses, governments and institutions, facilitating the sale of their products or services to other companies or organizations that in turn resell them, use them as components in products or services they offer _____ is also called business-to-_____ for short. (Note that while marketing to government entities shares some of the same dynamics of organizational marketing, B2G Marketing is meaningfully different.)
a. Business marketing
b. Marketspace
c. Customer franchise
d. Buy one, get one free

35. The general definition of an _____ is an evaluation of a person, organization, system, process, project or product. _____s are performed to ascertain the validity and reliability of information; also to provide an assessment of a system's internal control. The goal of an _____ is to express an opinion on the person/organization/system (etc) in question, under evaluation based on work done on a test basis.
a. ADTECH
b. AMAX
c. ACNielsen
d. Audit

36. _____ is a term used by marketing professionals to describe the analysis and improvement of the efficiency and effectiveness of marketing. This is accomplished by focus on the alignment of marketing activities, strategies, and metrics with business goals. It involves the creation a metrics framework to monitor marketing performance, and then develop and utilize marketing dashboards to manage marketing performance.
a. Marketing performance measurement and management
b. Commercial planning
c. Product naming
d. Business marketing

## Chapter 3. The Marketing Environment

1. _____ is defined by the American _____ Association as the activity, set of institutions, and processes for creating, communicating, delivering, and exchanging offerings that have value for customers, clients, partners, and society at large. The term developed from the original meaning which referred literally to going to market, as in shopping, or going to a market to sell goods or services.

_____ practice tends to be seen as a creative industry, which includes advertising, distribution and selling.

- a. Gatefold
- b. Business marketing
- c. Product naming
- d. Marketing

2. The _____ is a marketing term and refers to all of the forces outside of marketing that affect marketing management's ability to build and maintain successful relationships with target customers. The _____ consists of both the macroenvironment and the microenvironment.

The microenvironment refers to the forces that are close to the company and affect its ability to serve its customers.

- a. Brochure
- b. Marketing performance measurement and management
- c. Vertical market
- d. Market environment

3. The cost advantages of using _____ include:

- Reconciling conflicting preferences of lenders and borrowers

- Risk aversion- intermediaries help spread out and decrease the risks

- Economies of scale- using _____ reduces the costs of lending and borrowing

- Economies of scope- intermediaries concentrate on the demands of the lenders and borrowers and are able to enhance their products and services (use same inputs to produce different outputs)

_____ include:

- Banks
- Building societies
- Credit unions
- Financial advisers or brokers
- Insurance companies
- Collective investment schemes
- Pension funds

Financial institutions (intermediaries) perform the vital role of bringing together those economic agents with surplus funds who want to lend, with those with a shortage of funds who want to borrow.

## Chapter 3. The Marketing Environment

In doing this they offer the major benefits of maturity and risk transformation. It is possible for this to be done by direct contact between the ultimate borrowers, but there are major cost disadvantages of direct finance.

Indeed, one explanation of the existence of specialist _____ is that they have a related (cost) advantage in offering financial services, which not only enables them to make profit, but also raises the overall efficiency of the economy.

- a. 180SearchAssistant
- b. Power III
- c. 6-3-5 Brainwriting
- d. Financial intermediaries

4. A _____ is a company or individual that purchases goods or services with the intention of reselling them rather than consuming or using them. This is usually done for profit (but could be resold at a loss.) One example can be found in the industry of telecommunications, where companies buy excess amounts of transmission capacity or call time from other carriers and resell it to smaller carriers.
    - a. Mass market
    - b. Refusal to deal
    - c. Micromarketing
    - d. Reseller

5. A supply chain is the system of organizations, people, technology, activities, information and resources involved in moving a product or service from _____ to customer. Supply chain activities transform natural resources, raw materials and components into a finished product that is delivered to the end customer. In sophisticated supply chain systems, used products may re-enter the supply chain at any point where residual value is recyclable.
    - a. Supplier
    - b. Relationship Management Application
    - c. GE matrix
    - d. Little value placed on potential benefits

6. _____ is one of the four elements of marketing mix. An organization or set of organizations (go-betweens) involved in the process of making a product or service available for use or consumption by a consumer or business user.

The other three parts of the marketing mix are product, pricing, and promotion.

- a. Clustering
- b. LIFO
- c. Better Living Through Chemistry
- d. Distribution

7. _____ is a measure of the strength of a brand, product, service relative to competitive offerings. There is often a geographic element to the competitive landscape. In defining _____, you must see to what extent a product, brand, or firm controls a product category in a given geographic area.
    - a. Market dominance
    - b. Discretionary spending
    - c. Productivity
    - d. Market system

8. _____ is the management of the flow of goods, information and other resources, including energy and people, between the point of origin and the point of consumption in order to meet the requirements of consumers (frequently, and originally, military organizations.) _____ involves the integration of information, transportation, inventory, warehousing, material-handling, and packaging. _____ is a channel of the supply chain which adds the value of time and place utility.
    - a. Power III
    - b. 180SearchAssistant
    - c. 6-3-5 Brainwriting
    - d. Logistics

## Chapter 3. The Marketing Environment

9. _____ is an advertisement in which a particular product specifically mentions a competitor by name for the express purpose of showing why the competitor is inferior to the product naming it.

This should not be confused with parody advertisements, where a fictional product is being advertised for the purpose of poking fun at the particular advertisement, nor should it be confused with the use of a coined brand name for the purpose of comparing the product without actually naming an actual competitor. ('Wikipedia tastes better and is less filling than the Encyclopedia Galactica.')

In the 1980s, during what has been referred to as the cola wars, soft-drink manufacturer Pepsi ran a series of advertisements where people, caught on hidden camera, in a blind taste test, chose Pepsi over rival Coca-Cola.

a. Heavy-up
b. Comparative advertising
c. GL-70
d. Cost per conversion

10. _____ is a broad label that refers to any individuals or households that use goods and services generated within the economy. The concept of a _____ is used in different contexts, so that the usage and significance of the term may vary.

A _____ is a person who uses any product or service.

a. 180SearchAssistant
b. 6-3-5 Brainwriting
c. Power III
d. Consumer

11. _____ or _____ data refers to selected population characteristics as used in government, marketing or opinion research, or the _____ profiles used in such research. Note the distinction from the term 'demography' Commonly-used _____ include race, age, income, disabilities, mobility (in terms of travel time to work or number of vehicles available), educational attainment, home ownership, employment status, and even location.

a. Albert Einstein
b. AStore
c. African Americans
d. Demographic

12. _____ is a term used to describe a person who was born during the demographic Post-World War II baby boom. Many analysts now believe that two distinct cultural generations were born during this baby boom; the older generation is often called the Baby Boom Generation and the younger generation is often called Generation Jones. The term '_____' is sometimes used in a cultural context, and sometimes used to describe someone who was born during the post-WWII baby boom.

a. Generation Y
b. Greatest Generation
c. AStore
d. Baby boomer

13. _____ is a term used to identify people born after the post-World War II increase in birth rates (the baby boom) The term has been used in demography, the social sciences, and marketing, though it is most often used in popular culture.

In the U.S. _____ was originally referred to as the 'baby bust' generation because of the drop in the birth rate following the baby boom.

In the UK the term was first used in a 1964 study of British youth by Jane Deverson.

a. Generation Y  
c. Generation X  
b. AStore  
d. Greatest Generation

14. _____ is a cohort which consists of those people born after the Generation X cohort. Its name is controversial and is synonymous with several alternative names including The Net Generation, Millennials, Echo Boomers, and iGeneration. _____ consists primarily of the offspring of the Generation Jones and Baby Boomers cohorts.
   a. AStore  
   c. Greatest Generation  
   b. Generation X  
   d. Generation Y

15. In calculus, a function f defined on a subset of the real numbers with real values is called _____, if for all x and y such that x ≤ y one has f(x) ≤ f(y), so f preserves the order. In layman's terms, the sign of the slope is always positive (the curve tending upwards) or zero (i.e., non-decreasing, or asymptotic, or depicted as a horizontal, flat line) Likewise, a function is called monotonically decreasing (non-increasing) if, whenever x ≤ y, then f(x) ≥ f(y), so it reverses the order.
   a. 6-3-5 Brainwriting  
   c. Power III  
   b. 180SearchAssistant  
   d. Monotonic

16. _____ is a form of communication that typically attempts to persuade potential customers to purchase or to consume more of a particular brand of product or service. 'While now central to the contemporary global economy and the reproduction of global production networks, it is only quite recently that _____ has been more than a marginal influence on patterns of sales and production. The formation of modern _____ was intimately bound up with the emergence of new forms of monopoly capitalism around the end of the 19th and beginning of the 20th century as one element in corporate strategies to create, organize and where possible control markets, especially for mass produced consumer goods.
   a. Advertising  
   c. ACNielsen  
   b. AMAX  
   d. ADTECH

17. A _____ is a collection of symbols, experiences and associations connected with a product, a service, a person or any other artifact or entity.

   _____s have become increasingly important components of culture and the economy, now being described as 'cultural accessories and personal philosophies'.

   Some people distinguish the psychological aspect of a _____ from the experiential aspect.

   a. Naming rights  
   c. Brand  
   b. Status brand  
   d. Lovemarks

18. Procter is a surname, and may also refer to:

   - Bryan Waller Procter (pseud. Barry Cornwall), English poet
   - Goodwin Procter, American law firm
   - _____, consumer products multinational

   a. Comparison-Shopping agent  
   c. Developed country  
   b. Procter ' Gamble  
   d. Push

## Chapter 3. The Marketing Environment

19. _____s is the social science that studies the production, distribution, and consumption of goods and services. The term _____s comes from the Ancient Greek oá¼°κονομἷα from oá¼¶κος (oikos, 'house') + vÏŒμος (nomos, 'custom' or 'law'), hence 'rules of the house(hold)'. Current _____ models developed out of the broader field of political economy in the late 19th century, owing to a desire to use an empirical approach more akin to the physical sciences.
   a. ADTECH
   b. Industrial organization
   c. ACNielsen
   d. Economic

20. In economics, _____ is how a nation's total economy is distributed among its population. ._____ has always been a central concern of economic theory and economic policy. Classical economists such as Adam Smith, Thomas Malthus and David Ricardo were mainly concerned with factor _____, that is, the distribution of income between the main factors of production, land, labour and capital.
   a. Inflation rate
   b. ACNielsen
   c. Internality
   d. Income distribution

21. A personal and cultural _____ is a relative ethic _____, an assumption upon which implementation can be extrapolated. A _____ system is a set of consistent _____s and measures that is soo not true. A principle _____ is a foundation upon which other _____s and measures of integrity are based.
   a. Dolly Dimples
   b. Private branding
   c. Customization
   d. Value

22. A _____ is something that is acted upon or used by or by human labour or industry, for use as a building material to create some product or structure. Often the term is used to denote material that came from nature and is in an unprocessed or minimally processed state. Iron ore, logs, and crude oil, would be examples.
   a. Raw material
   b. 180SearchAssistant
   c. Power III
   d. 6-3-5 Brainwriting

23. _____ is the use of an object (typically referred to as an RFID tag) applied to or incorporated into a product, animal, or person for the purpose of identification and tracking using radio waves. Some tags can be read from several meters away and beyond the line of sight of the reader.

Most RFID tags contain at least two parts.

   a. 180SearchAssistant
   b. Power III
   c. 6-3-5 Brainwriting
   d. Radio-frequency identification

24. The United States _____ is an independent agency of the United States government created in 1972 through the Consumer Product Safety Act to protect 'against unreasonable risks of injuries associated with consumer products.' As of 2006 its acting chairman is Nancy Nord, a Republican. The other commissioner is Thomas Hill Moore, a Democrat. Normally the board has three commissioners.
   a. 6-3-5 Brainwriting
   b. 180SearchAssistant
   c. Power III
   d. Consumer Product Safety Commission

25. The _____ is an economic and political union of 27 member states, located primarily in Europe. It was established by the Treaty of Maastricht on 1 November 1993 upon the foundations of the pre-existing European Economic Community. With almost 500 million citizens, the _____ combined generates an estimated 30% share (US$16.8 trillion in 2007) of the nominal gross world product.

a. Eurozone
b. ACNielsen
c. ADTECH
d. European Union

26. The U.S. _____ is an agency of the United States Department of Health and Human Services and is responsible for regulating and supervising the safety of foods, dietary supplements, drugs, vaccines, biological medical products, blood products, medical devices, radiation-emitting devices, veterinary products, and cosmetics. The FDA also enforces section 361 of the Public Health Service Act and the associated regulations, including sanitation requirements on interstate travel as well as specific rules for control of disease on products ranging from pet turtles to semen donations for assisted reproductive medicine techniques.

The FDA is an agency within the United States Department of Health and Human Services responsible for protecting and promoting the nation's public health.

a. Food and Drug Administration
b. Power III
c. 6-3-5 Brainwriting
d. 180SearchAssistant

27. The phrase _____, according to the Organization for Economic Co-operation and Development, refers to 'creative work undertaken on a systematic basis in order to increase the stock of knowledge, including knowledge of man, culture and society, and the use of this stock of knowledge to devise new applications [sic]' Though it is questionable that an organization is needed for this definition, as it is quite obvious that _____ refers to the _____ of something.

New product design and development is more often than not a crucial factor in the survival of a company. In an industry that is fast changing, firms must continually revise their design and range of products.

a. 6-3-5 Brainwriting
b. Power III
c. Research and development
d. 180SearchAssistant

28. _____ refers to 'controlling human or societal behaviour by rules or restrictions.' _____ can take many forms: legal restrictions promulgated by a government authority, self-_____, social _____, co-_____ and market _____. One can consider _____ as actions of conduct imposing sanctions (such as a fine.) This action of administrative law, or implementing regulatory law, may be contrasted with statutory or case law.

a. Consumer protection
b. Robinson-Patman Act
c. Nutrition Labeling and Education Act
d. Regulation

29. The _____ is an independent agency of the United States government, established in 1914 by the _____ Act. Its principal mission is the promotion of 'consumer protection' and the elimination and prevention of what regulators perceive to be harmfully 'anti-competitive' business practices, such as coercive monopoly.

The _____ Act was one of President Wilson's major acts against trusts.

a. 180SearchAssistant
b. 6-3-5 Brainwriting
c. Power III
d. Federal Trade Commission

## Chapter 3. The Marketing Environment

30. _____ refers to a type of marketing involving the cooperative efforts of a 'for profit' business and a non-profit organization for mutual benefit. The term is sometimes used more broadly and generally to refer to any type of marketing effort for social and other charitable causes, including in-house marketing efforts by non-profit organizations. Cause marketing differs from corporate giving (philanthropy) as the latter generally involves a specific donation that is tax deductible, while cause marketing is a marketing relationship generally not based on a donation.
   - a. Diversity marketing
   - b. Guerrilla Marketing
   - c. Global marketing
   - d. Cause-related marketing

31. _____ is a branch of philosophy which seeks to address questions about morality, such as how a moral outcome can be achieved in a specific situation (applied _____), how moral values should be determined (normative _____), what moral values people actually abide by (descriptive _____), what the fundamental semantic, ontological, and epistemic nature of _____ or morality is (meta-_____), and how moral capacity or moral agency develops and what its nature is (moral psychology.)

Socrates was one of the first Greek philosophers to encourage both scholars and the common citizen to turn their attention from the outside world to the condition of man. In this view, Knowledge having a bearing on human life was placed highest, all other knowledge being secondary.
   - a. AMAX
   - b. ACNielsen
   - c. Ethics
   - d. ADTECH

32. The _____ is an independent agency of the United States government, created, directed, and empowered by Congressional statute , and with the majority of its commissioners appointed by the current President.
   - a. Federal Communications Commission
   - b. 6-3-5 Brainwriting
   - c. Power III
   - d. 180SearchAssistant

33. Regulation refers to 'controlling human or societal behaviour by rules or restrictions.' Regulation can take many forms: legal restrictions promulgated by a government authority, self-regulation, social regulation (e.g. norms), co-regulation and market regulation. One can consider regulation as actions of conduct imposing sanctions (such as a fine.) This action of administrative law, or implementing _____ law, may be contrasted with statutory or case law.
   - a. Federal Food, Drug, and Cosmetic Act
   - b. Community Trade Mark
   - c. Gripe site
   - d. Regulatory

34. _____ is a sub-discipline and type of marketing. There are two main definitional characteristics which distinguish it from other types of marketing. The first is that it attempts to send its messages directly to consumers, without the use of intervening media.
   - a. Power III
   - b. Database marketing
   - c. Direct Marketing Associations
   - d. Direct marketing

35. _____ is the practice of individuals including commercial businesses, governments and institutions, facilitating the sale of their products or services to other companies or organizations that in turn resell them, use them as components in products or services they offer _____ is also called business-to-_____ for short. (Note that while marketing to government entities shares some of the same dynamics of organizational marketing, B2G Marketing is meaningfully different.)

## Chapter 3. The Marketing Environment

a. Buy one, get one free
c. Customer franchise
b. Marketspace
d. Business marketing

36. _____ was originally coined by Austrian psychologist Alfred Adler in 1929. The current broader sense of the word dates from 1961.

In sociology, a _____ is the way a person lives.

a. Power III
c. 6-3-5 Brainwriting
b. Lifestyle
d. 180SearchAssistant

37. _____ is a demographic defining a particular market segment related to sustainable living, 'green' ecological initiatives, and generally composed of a relatively upscale and well-educated population segment. Researchers have reported a range of sizes of the _____ market segment. For example, Worldwatch Institute reported that the _____ market segment in the year 2006 was estimated at $300 billion, approximately 30% of the USA consumer market; and, a study by the Natural Marketing Institute showed that in 2007, 40 million Americans were included within the _____ demographic.

a. Black PRies
c. Lifestyles of health and sustainability
b. PlattForm, Inc.
d. Positioning

## Chapter 4. Managing Marketing Information

1. _____ is defined by the American _____ Association as the activity, set of institutions, and processes for creating, communicating, delivering, and exchanging offerings that have value for customers, clients, partners, and society at large. The term developed from the original meaning which referred literally to going to market, as in shopping, or going to a market to sell goods or services.

_____ practice tends to be seen as a creative industry, which includes advertising, distribution and selling.

a. Business marketing
b. Product naming
c. Marketing
d. Gatefold

2. _____ , according to Cornish, 'the process of acquiring and analyzing information in order to understand the market (both existing and potential customers); to determine the current and future needs and preferences, attitudes and behavior of the market; and to assess changes in the business environment that may affect the size and nature of the market in the future.' ('Product', 1997, p147.)

This figure shows how the interaction between variables from producers, communication channels, and consumers vary the effectiveness of _____ which affects the performance of the sales of a new product. The product is central in a circle because it helps to direct what information is gathered and how.

a. Specialty catalogs
b. Brand parity
c. Market intelligence
d. Co-branding

3. A _____ is a structured collection of records or data that is stored in a computer system. The structure is achieved by organizing the data according to a _____ model. The model in most common use today is the relational model.

a. Power III
b. Database
c. 6-3-5 Brainwriting
d. 180SearchAssistant

4. _____ is a popular searchable archive of content from newspapers, magazines, legal documents and other printed sources. _____ claims to be the 'world's largest collection of public records, unpublished opinions, forms, legal, news, and business information' while offering their products to a wide range of professionals in the legal, risk management, corporate, government, law enforcement, accounting and academic markets. Typical customers of _____ include lawyers, law students, journalists, and academics.

a. 180SearchAssistant
b. 6-3-5 Brainwriting
c. LexisNexis
d. Power III

5. A _____ is a set of exclusive rights granted by a State to an inventor or his assignee for a limited period of time in exchange for a disclosure of an invention.

The procedure for granting _____s, the requirements placed on the _____ee and the extent of the exclusive rights vary widely between countries according to national laws and international agreements. Typically, however, a _____ application must include one or more claims defining the invention which must be new, inventive, and useful or industrially applicable.

a. Non-conventional trademark
b. Patent
c. Denominazione di origine controllata
d. Wheeler-Lea Act

## Chapter 4. Managing Marketing Information

6. Procter is a surname, and may also refer to:

- Bryan Waller Procter (pseud. Barry Cornwall), English poet
- Goodwin Procter, American law firm
- _____, consumer products multinational

a. Push  
c. Procter ' Gamble  
b. Comparison-Shopping agent  
d. Developed country

7. A _____ or trade mark, identified by the symbols â„¢ (not yet registered) and Â® (registered) business organization or other legal entity to identify that the products and/or services to consumers with which the _____ appears originate from a unique source of origin, and to distinguish its products or services from those of other entities. A _____ is a type of intellectual property, and typically a name, word, phrase, logo, symbol, design, image, or a combination of these elements. There is also a range of non-conventional _____ s comprising marks which do not fall into these standard categories.

a. Risk management  
c. Power III  
b. 180SearchAssistant  
d. Trademark

8. The _____ is an agency in the United States Department of Commerce that issues patents to inventors and businesses for their inventions, and trademark registration for product and intellectual property identification.

The USPTO is currently based in Alexandria, Virginia, after a 2006 move from the Crystal City area of Arlington, Virginia. The offices under Patents and the Chief Information Officer that remained just outside the southern end of Crystal City completed moving to Randolph Square, a brand new building in Shirlington Village, on 27 April 2009.

a. Underwriters Laboratories  
c. United States Patent and Trademark Office  
b. INVISTA  
d. Access Commerce

9. Consumer market research is a form of applied sociology that concentrates on understanding the behaviours, whims and preferences, of consumers in a market-based economy, and aims to understand the effects and comparative success of marketing campaigns. The field of consumer _____ as a statistical science was pioneered by Arthur Nielsen with the founding of the ACNielsen Company in 1923 .

Thus _____ is the systematic and objective identification, collection, analysis, and dissemination of information for the purpose of assisting management in decision making related to the identification and solution of problems and opportunities in marketing.

a. Market analysis  
c. Logit analysis  
b. Simple random sampling  
d. Marketing research

10. _____ refer to a collection of facts usually collected as the result of experience, observation or experiment or a set of premises. This may consist of numbers, words particularly as measurements or observations of a set of variables. _____ are often viewed as a lowest level of abstraction from which information and knowledge are derived.

a. Median  
b. Randomization  
c. P-Value  
d. Data

11. _____ is a term used to describe a process of preparing and collecting data - for example as part of a process improvement or similar project.

_____ usually takes place early on in an improvement project, and is often formalised through a _____ Plan which often contains the following activity.

1. Pre collection activity - Agree goals, target data, definitions, methods
2. Collection - _____
3. Present Findings - usually involves some form of sorting analysis and/or presentation.

A formal _____ process is necessary as it ensures that data gathered is both defined and accurate and that subsequent decisions based on arguments embodied in the findings are valid . The process provides both a baseline from which to measure from and in certain cases a target on what to improve. Types of _____ 1-By mail questionnaires 2-By personal interview

- Six sigma
- Sampling (statistics)

a. 180SearchAssistant  
b. Data collection  
c. 6-3-5 Brainwriting  
d. Power III

12. _____ describes data and characteristics about the population or phenomenon being studied. _____ answers the questions who, what, where, when and how.

Although the data description is factual, accurate and systematic, the research cannot describe what caused a situation.

a. Sampling error  
b. Varimax rotation  
c. Power III  
d. Descriptive research

13. _____ is a type of research conducted because a problem has not been clearly defined. _____ helps determine the best research design, data collection method and selection of subjects. Given its fundamental nature, _____ often concludes that a perceived problem does not actually exist.

a. ACNielsen  
b. Intent scale translation  
c. IDDEA  
d. Exploratory research

14. _____ is a term for unprocessed data, it is also known as primary data. It is a relative term _____ can be input to a computer program or used in manual analysis procedures such as gathering statistics from a survey.

a. Product manager  
b. Chief marketing officer  
c. Shoppers Food ' Pharmacy  
d. Raw data

## Chapter 4. Managing Marketing Information

15. Combining Existing _____ Sources with New Primary Data Sources

Imagine that we could get hold of a good collection of surveys taken in earlier years, such as detailed studies about changes going on in this phase and hopefully additional studies in the years to come. Analyzing this data base over time could give us a good picture of what changes actually have taken place in the orientation of the population and of the extent to which new technical concepts did have an impact on subgroups of the population. Furthermore, data archives can help to prepare studies on change over time by monitoring what questions have been asked in earlier years and alerting principal investigators to important questions which should be repeated in planned research projects.

   a. 180SearchAssistant  
   b. 6-3-5 Brainwriting  
   c. Power III  
   d. Secondary data

16. _____ is a global marketing research firm, with worldwide headquarters in New York City. Regional headquarters for North America are located in Schaumburg, IL. As of 2008, its the part of The Nielsen Company.

   a. E-Detailing  
   b. Alloy Entertainment  
   c. InfoNU  
   d. ACNielsen

17. _____ is a form of communication that typically attempts to persuade potential customers to purchase or to consume more of a particular brand of product or service. 'While now central to the contemporary global economy and the reproduction of global production networks, it is only quite recently that _____ has been more than a marginal influence on patterns of sales and production. The formation of modern _____ was intimately bound up with the emergence of new forms of monopoly capitalism around the end of the 19th and beginning of the 20th century as one element in corporate strategies to create, organize and where possible control markets, especially for mass produced consumer goods.

   a. ADTECH  
   b. AMAX  
   c. ACNielsen  
   d. Advertising

18. _____ is a radio audience research company in the United States which collects listener data on radio audiences similar to that collected by Nielsen Media Research on television audiences. It was founded as American Research Bureau by Jim Seiler in 1949 and became bi-coastal by merging with L.A. based Coffin, Cooper and Clay in the early 1950s. ARB's initial business was the collection of television broadcast ratings exclusively.

   a. Arbitron  
   b. Access Commerce  
   c. American Cancer Society  
   d. American Heart Association

19. The United States _____ is the government agency that is responsible for the United States Census. It also gathers other national demographic and economic data.

   a. 6-3-5 Brainwriting  
   b. 180SearchAssistant  
   c. Census Bureau  
   d. Power III

20. _____ is a telephone surveying technique in which the interviewer follows a script provided by a software application. The software is able to customize the flow of the questionnaire based on the answers provided, as well as information already known about the participant.

## Chapter 4. Managing Marketing Information

CATI may function in the following manner

- A computerized questionnaire is administered to respondents over the telephone.
- The interviewer sits in front of a computer screen
- Upon command, the computer dials the telephone number to be called.
- When contact is made, the interviewer reads the questions posed on the computer screen and records the respondent's answers directly into the computer.
- Interim and update reports can be compiled instantaneously, as the data are being collected.
- CATI software has built-in logic, which also enhances data accuracy.
- The program will personalize questions and control for logically incorrect answers, such as percentage answers that do not add up to 100 percent.
- The software has built-in branching logic, which will skip questions that are not applicable or will probe for more detail when warranted.

a. 6-3-5 Brainwriting
b. Computer-assisted telephone interviewing
c. Power III
d. 180SearchAssistant

21. _____ or _____ data refers to selected population characteristics as used in government, marketing or opinion research, or the _____ profiles used in such research. Note the distinction from the term 'demography' Commonly-used _____ include race, age, income, disabilities, mobility (in terms of travel time to work or number of vehicles available), educational attainment, home ownership, employment status, and even location.

a. Demographic
b. AStore
c. Albert Einstein
d. African Americans

22. The _____ is an independent agency of the United States government, established in 1914 by the _____ Act. Its principal mission is the promotion of 'consumer protection' and the elimination and prevention of what regulators perceive to be harmfully 'anti-competitive' business practices, such as coercive monopoly.

The _____ Act was one of President Wilson's major acts against trusts.

a. Power III
b. 6-3-5 Brainwriting
c. 180SearchAssistant
d. Federal Trade Commission

23. _____ uses online or offline interactive media to communicate with consumers and to promote products, brands, services, and public service announcements, corporate or political groups.

In the inaugural issue of the Journal of _____ , editors Li and Leckenby (2000) defined _____ as the 'paid and unpaid presentation and promotion of products, services and ideas by an identified sponsor through mediated means involving mutual action between consumers and producers.' This is most commonly performed through the Internet as a medium.

It is these mutual actions or interactions that enhance what _____ is trying to achieve.

a. Enterprise Search Marketing  
b. Audience Screening  
c. Internet currency  
d. Interactive Advertising

24. _____ often refers to either primary or secondary research. Secondary research involves a company using information compiled from various sources, which is about a new or existing product. The advantages of secondary research are that it is relatively cheap and easily accessible.

a. Mystery shoppers  
b. Mystery shopping  
c. Questionnaire  
d. Market Research

25. The U.S. _____ is an independent agency of the United States government which holds primary responsibility for enforcing the federal securities laws and regulating the securities industry, the nation's stock and options exchanges, and other electronic securities markets. The SEC was created by section 4 of the Securities Exchange Act of 1934 (now codified as 15 U.S.C. Â§ 78d and commonly referred to as the 1934 Act.)

a. Power III  
b. 6-3-5 Brainwriting  
c. Securities and Exchange Commission  
d. 180SearchAssistant

26. A _____ is a business that is independently owned and operated, with a small number of employees and relatively low volume of sales. The legal definition of 'small' often varies by country and industry, but is generally under 100 employees in the United States and under 50 employees in the European Union. In comparison, the definition of mid-sized business by the number of employees is generally under 500 in the U.S. and 250 for the European Union.

a. Time to market  
b. Business stature  
c. Chain stores  
d. Small Business

27. The _____ is a United States government agency that provides support to small businesses.

The mission of the _____ is 'to maintain and strengthen the nation's economy by enabling the establishment and viability of small businesses and by assisting in the economic recovery of communities after disasters.'

The _____ makes loans directly to businesses and acts as a guarantor on bank loans. In some circumstances it also makes loans to victims of natural disasters, works to get government procurement contracts for small businesses, and assists businesses with management, technical and training issues.

a. Small Business Administration  
b. Power III  
c. 6-3-5 Brainwriting  
d. 180SearchAssistant

28. _____ in organizations and public policy is both the organizational process of creating and maintaining a plan; and the psychological process of thinking about the activities required to create a desired goal on some scale. As such, it is a fundamental property of intelligent behavior. This thought process is essential to the creation and refinement of a plan, or integration of it with other plans, that is, it combines forecasting of developments with the preparation of scenarios of how to react to them.

a. 6-3-5 Brainwriting  
b. Planning  
c. Power III  
d. 180SearchAssistant

29. In marketing and the social sciences, _____ is a social research technique that involves the direct observation of phenomena in their natural setting. This differentiates it from experimental research in which a quasi-artificial environment is created to control for spurious factors, and where at least one of the variables is manipulated as part of the experiment.

## Chapter 4. Managing Marketing Information

Compared with quantitative research and experimental research, _____ tends to be less reliable but often more valid.

a. ADTECH  
c. ACNielsen  
b. AMAX  
d. Observational Research

30. _____ a research method involving the use of questionnaires and/or statistical surveys to gather data about people and their thoughts and behaviours.

a. Stratified sampling  
c. Randomization  
b. Control chart  
d. Survey Research

31. A _____ is a research instrument consisting of a series of questions and other prompts for the purpose of gathering information from respondents. Although they are often designed for statistical analysis of the responses, this is not always the case. The _____ was invented by Sir Francis Galton.

a. Mystery shopping  
c. Mystery shoppers  
b. Questionnaire  
d. Market research

32. A _____ is a form of qualitative research in which a group of people are asked about their attitude towards a product, service, concept, advertisement, idea, or packaging. Questions are asked in an interactive group setting where participants are free to talk with other group members.

Ernest Dichter originated the idea of having a 'group therapy' for products and this process is what became known as a _____.

a. Focus group  
c. Preference regression  
b. Simple random sampling  
d. Market analysis

33. _____, also referred to as i-marketing, web marketing, online marketing is the marketing of products or services over the Internet.

The Internet has brought many unique benefits to marketing, one of which being lower costs for the distribution of information and media to a global audience. The interactive nature of _____, both in terms of providing instant response and eliciting responses, is a unique quality of the medium.

a. ADTECH  
c. ACNielsen  
b. Internet marketing  
d. AMAX

34. _____ are used to collect information and gain feedback via the telephone and the internet. _____ are used for customer research purposes by call centres for customer relationship management and performance management purposes. They are also used for political polling, market research and job satisfaction surveying.

a. Intangibility  
c. Individual branding  
b. Engagement  
d. Automated surveys

35. _____ is a way of expressing knowledge or belief that an event will occur or has occurred. In mathematics the concept has been given an exact meaning in _____ theory, that is used extensively in such areas of study as mathematics, statistics, finance, gambling, science, and philosophy to draw conclusions about the likelihood of potential events and the underlying mechanics of complex systems.

a. Probability  
c. Mean  
b. Correlation  
d. Standard score

36. A sample is a subject chosen from a population for investigation. A _____ is one chosen by a method involving an unpredictable component. Random sampling can also refer to taking a number of independent observations from the same probability distribution, without involving any real population.

a. 180SearchAssistant  
c. Selection bias  
b. Power III  
d. Random sample

37. The _____ of a statistical sample is the number of observations that constitute it. It is typically denoted n, a positive integer (natural number.)

Typically, all else being equal, a larger _____ leads to increased precision in estimates of various properties of the population.

a. Statistics  
c. Sample size  
b. Control chart  
d. Statistical inference

38. _____ is that part of statistical practice concerned with the selection of individual observations intended to yield some knowledge about a population of concern, especially for the purposes of statistical inference. Each observation measures one or more properties (weight, location, etc.) of an observable entity enumerated to distinguish objects or individuals.

a. Richard Buckminster 'Bucky' Fuller  
c. AStore  
b. Sports Marketing Group  
d. Sampling

39. _____ is an American firm that measures media audiences, including television, radio, theatre films (via the AMC MAP program) and newspapers. _____, headquartered in New York City and operating primarily from Chicago, is best-known for the Nielsen Ratings, a measurement of television viewership.

_____, the preeminent media research company in the world, began as a division of ACNielsen, a marketing research firm.

a. Superbrands  
c. Zany Brainy  
b. Coinstar  
d. Nielsen Media Research

40. A _____ is a tool used to measure the viewing habits of TV and cable audiences.

The _____ is a 'box', about the size of a paperback book. The box is hooked up to each television set and is accompanied by a remote control unit.

## Chapter 4. Managing Marketing Information

a. Power III
b. 6-3-5 Brainwriting
c. People meter
d. 180SearchAssistant

41. _____ is the realization of an application idea, model, design, specification, standard, algorithm an _____ is a realization of a technical specification or algorithm as a program, software component, or other computer system. Many _____s may exist for a given specification or standard.
a. AMAX
b. ADTECH
c. ACNielsen
d. Implementation

42. _____ consists of the processes a company uses to track and organize its contacts with its current and prospective customers. _____ software is used to support these processes; information about customers and customer interactions can be entered, stored and accessed by employees in different company departments. Typical _____ goals are to improve services provided to customers, and to use customer contact information for targeted marketing.
a. Social marketing
b. Customer franchise
c. Buy one, get one free
d. Customer relationship management

43. Customer _____ consists of the processes a company uses to track and organize its contacts with its current and prospective customers. CRelationship management software is used to support these processes; information about customers and customer interactions can be entered, stored and accessed by employees in different company departments. Typical CRelationship management goals are to improve services provided to customers, and to use customer contact information for targeted marketing.
a. Corporate image
b. Kano model
c. Pinstorm
d. Relationship management

44. _____ is the process of extracting hidden patterns from data. As more data is gathered, with the amount of data doubling every three years, _____ is becoming an increasingly important tool to transform this data into information. It is commonly used in a wide range of profiling practices, such as marketing, surveillance, fraud detection and scientific discovery.
a. 180SearchAssistant
b. Structure mining
c. Data mining
d. Power III

45. A _____ is a commercial building for storage of goods. _____s are used by manufacturers, importers, exporters, wholesalers, transport businesses, customs, etc. They are usually large plain buildings in industrial areas of cities and towns.
a. 6-3-5 Brainwriting
b. 180SearchAssistant
c. Power III
d. Warehouse

46. An _____ is a private network that uses Internet protocols, network connectivity, and possibly the public telecommunication system to securely share part of an organization's information or operations with suppliers, vendors, partners, customers or other businesses. An _____ can be viewed as part of a company's intranet that is extended to users outside the company (e.g.: normally over the Internet.) It has also been described as a 'state of mind' in which the Internet is perceived as a way to do business with a preapproved set of other companies business-to-business (B2B), in isolation from all other Internet users.

a. AMAX  
b. ADTECH  
c. Extranet  
d. ACNielsen

47. _____ is the practice of individuals including commercial businesses, governments and institutions, facilitating the sale of their products or services to other companies or organizations that in turn resell them, use them as components in products or services they offer _____ is also called business-to-_____ for short. (Note that while marketing to government entities shares some of the same dynamics of organizational marketing, B2G Marketing is meaningfully different.)

a. Buy one, get one free  
b. Customer franchise  
c. Business marketing  
d. Marketspace

48. _____s is the social science that studies the production, distribution, and consumption of goods and services. The term _____s comes from the Ancient Greek οἰκονομία from οἶκος (oikos, 'house') + νόμος (nomos, 'custom' or 'law'), hence 'rules of the house(hold)'. Current _____ models developed out of the broader field of political economy in the late 19th century, owing to a desire to use an empirical approach more akin to the physical sciences.

a. ACNielsen  
b. ADTECH  
c. Industrial organization  
d. Economic

49. The Oxford University Press defines _____ as 'marketing on a worldwide scale reconciling or taking commercial advantage of global operational differences, similarities and opportunities in order to meet global objectives.' Oxford University Press' Glossary of Marketing Terms.

Here are three reasons for the shift from domestic to _____ as given by the authors of the textbook, _____ Management--3rd Edition by Masaaki Kotabe and Kristiaan Helsen, 2004.

One of the product categories in which global competition has been easy to track is in U.S. automotive sales.

a. Guerrilla Marketing  
b. Relationship marketing  
c. Global marketing  
d. Cause-related Marketing

50. _____ is a broad label that refers to any individuals or households that use goods and services generated within the economy. The concept of a _____ is used in different contexts, so that the usage and significance of the term may vary.

A _____ is a person who uses any product or service.

a. 6-3-5 Brainwriting  
b. Power III  
c. 180SearchAssistant  
d. Consumer

51. _____ laws and regulations seek to protect any individual from loss of privacy due to failures or limitations of corporate customer privacy measures. They recognize that the damage done by privacy loss is typically not measurable, nor can it be undone, and that commercial organizations have little or no interest in taking unprofitable measures to drastically increase privacy of customers - indeed, their motivation is very often quite the opposite, to share data for commercial advantage, and to fail to officially recognize it as sensitive, so as to avoid legal liability for lapses of security that may occur.

_____ concerns date back to the first commercial couriers and bankers, who in every culture took strong measures to protect customer privacy, but also in every culture tended to be subject to very harsh punitive measures for failures to keep a customer's information private.

a. Personalized marketing
b. Consumer privacy
c. Disintermediation
d. Consumer-to-consumer

52. _____ is a branch of philosophy which seeks to address questions about morality, such as how a moral outcome can be achieved in a specific situation (applied _____), how moral values should be determined (normative _____), what moral values people actually abide by (descriptive _____), what the fundamental semantic, ontological, and epistemic nature of _____ or morality is (meta-_____), and how moral capacity or moral agency develops and what its nature is (moral psychology.)

Socrates was one of the first Greek philosophers to encourage both scholars and the common citizen to turn their attention from the outside world to the condition of man. In this view, Knowledge having a bearing on human life was placed highest, all other knowledge being secondary.

a. AMAX
b. Ethics
c. ACNielsen
d. ADTECH

53. _____ is a sub-discipline and type of marketing. There are two main definitional characteristics which distinguish it from other types of marketing. The first is that it attempts to send its messages directly to consumers, without the use of intervening media.

a. Direct Marketing Associations
b. Direct marketing
c. Power III
d. Database marketing

54. _____ is the ability of an individual or group to seclude themselves or information about themselves and thereby reveal themselves selectively. The boundaries and content of what is considered private differ among cultures and individuals, but share basic common themes. _____ is sometimes related to anonymity, the wish to remain unnoticed or unidentified in the public realm.

a. 180SearchAssistant
b. 6-3-5 Brainwriting
c. Power III
d. Privacy

55. A _____ is a collection of symbols, experiences and associations connected with a product, a service, a person or any other artifact or entity.

_____s have become increasingly important components of culture and the economy, now being described as 'cultural accessories and personal philosophies'.

Some people distinguish the psychological aspect of a _____ from the experiential aspect.

a. Status brand
b. Naming rights
c. Lovemarks
d. Brand

## Chapter 4. Managing Marketing Information

56. The _____ is a senior level executive within a business or organization who is responsible for managing the risks and business impacts of privacy laws and policies. The _____ position is relatively new and was created to respond to both consumer concern over the use of personal information, including, but not limited to, medical data and financial information, and laws and regulations, including, but not limited to, legislation concerning the protection of patient medical records (e.g., The Health Insurance Portability and Accountability Act of 1996, or HIPAA) and the use and safeguarding of consumer financial and banking transactions (e.g., The Fair Credit Reporting Act and its Disposal Rule, and the Gramm-Leach-Bliley Act and its Safeguards Rule and Financial Privacy Rule).
    a. Chief privacy officer
    b. Soft sell
    c. Jobbing house
    d. Product innovation

57. _____ is the examining of goods or services from retailers with the intent to purchase at that time. _____ is an activity of selection and/or purchase. In some contexts it is considered a leisure activity as well as an economic one.
    a. Hawkers
    b. Khodebshchik
    c. Discount store
    d. Shopping

58. The _____ is a professional association for marketers. As of 2008 it had approximately 40,000 members. There are collegiate chapters on 250 campuses.
    a. American Marketing Association
    b. AMAX
    c. ADTECH
    d. ACNielsen

59. Founded in 1957, the _____ is one of the largest trade associations of market research and polling professionals. _____ has more than 3,000 members worldwide, representing all segments of the research industry. _____ advances, protects and promotes knowledge, standards, excellence, ethics, professional development and innovation for the global market and opinion research profession.
    a. 180SearchAssistant
    b. Power III
    c. PRSA
    d. Marketing Research Association

## Chapter 5. Consumer and Business Buyer Behavior

1. _____ is a broad label that refers to any individuals or households that use goods and services generated within the economy. The concept of a _____ is used in different contexts, so that the usage and significance of the term may vary.

A _____ is a person who uses any product or service.

a. Power III
b. Consumer
c. 6-3-5 Brainwriting
d. 180SearchAssistant

2. _____ is the study of when, why, how, where and what people do or do not buy products. It blends elements from psychology, sociology, social psychology, anthropology and economics. It attempts to understand the buyer decision making process, both individually and in groups. It studies characteristics of individual consumers such as demographics and behavioural variables in an attempt to understand people's wants. It also tries to assess influences on the consumer from groups such as family, friends, reference groups, and society in general.

a. Marketing buzz
b. Communal marketing
c. Shopping Neutral
d. Consumer behavior

3. _____ is difficult to define. For example, in 1952, Alfred Kroeber and Clyde Kluckhohn compiled a list of 164 definitions of '_____' in _____: A Critical Review of Concepts and Definitions. However, the word '_____' is most commonly used in three basic senses:

- excellence of taste in the fine arts and humanities
- an integrated pattern of human knowledge, belief, and behavior that depends upon the capacity for symbolic thought and social learning
- the set of shared attitudes, values, goals, and practices that characterizes an institution, organization or group.

When the concept first emerged in eighteenth- and nineteenth-century Europe, it connoted a process of cultivation or improvement, as in agriculture or horticulture. In the nineteenth century, it came to refer first to the betterment or refinement of the individual, especially through education, and then to the fulfillment of national aspirations or ideals.

a. African Americans
b. Albert Einstein
c. AStore
d. Culture

4. _____ is defined by the American _____ Association as the activity, set of institutions, and processes for creating, communicating, delivering, and exchanging offerings that have value for customers, clients, partners, and society at large. The term developed from the original meaning which referred literally to going to market, as in shopping, or going to a market to sell goods or services.

_____ practice tends to be seen as a creative industry, which includes advertising, distribution and selling.

a. Product naming
b. Gatefold
c. Business marketing
d. Marketing

# Chapter 5. Consumer and Business Buyer Behavior

5. Procter is a surname, and may also refer to:

- Bryan Waller Procter (pseud. Barry Cornwall), English poet
- Goodwin Procter, American law firm
- _____, consumer products multinational

   a. Comparison-Shopping agent            b. Push
   c. Procter ' Gamble                         d. Developed country

6. In sociology, anthropology and cultural studies, a _____ is a group of people with a culture (whether distinct or hidden) which differentiates them from the larger culture to which they belong. If a particular _____ is characterized by a systematic opposition to the dominant culture, it may be described as a counterculture. As Ken Gelder notes, _____s are social, with their own shared conventions, values and rituals, but they can also seem 'immersed' or self-absorbed--another feature that distinguishes them from countercultures.

   a. 6-3-5 Brainwriting                  b. Power III
   c. 180SearchAssistant               d. Subculture

7. A _____ is a party that mediates between a buyer and a seller. A _____ who also acts as a seller or as a buyer becomes a principal party to the deal. Distinguish agent: one who acts on behalf of a principal.

   a. 180SearchAssistant               b. Professional services
   c. Power III                               d. Broker

8. _____ is one of the oldest financial services firms in the world. It is a leader in financial services with assets of $2.3 trillion., and the largest market capitalization and deposit base of any U.S. banking institution.

   a. CoolBrands                       b. Consumers Union
   c. Coinstar                                  d. JPMorgan Chase ' Co.

9. _____ or simply buzz is a term used in word-of-mouth marketing. The interaction of consumers and users of a product or service serve to amplify the original marketing message.

Some describe buzz as a form of hype among consumers, a vague but positive association, excitement, or anticipation about a product or service.

   a. Marketing buzz                   b. Compliance professional
   c. Consumption smoothing         d. Shopping Neutral

10. _____ is an employment website owned by Monster Worldwide. Monster is one of the 20 most visited websites out of 100 million worldwide, according to comScore Media Metrics (November 2006.) It was created in 1999 by the merger of The Monster Board (TMB) and Online Career Center (OCC), which were two of the first and most popular career web sites on the Internet.

   a. Monster.com                      b. 6-3-5 Brainwriting
   c. Power III                              d. 180SearchAssistant

## Chapter 5. Consumer and Business Buyer Behavior

11. _____ involves disseminating information about a product, product line, brand, or company. It is one of the four key aspects of the marketing mix. (The other three elements are product marketing, pricing, and distribution). P>_____ is generally sub-divided into two parts:

- Above the line _____: Promotion in the media (e.g. TV, radio, newspapers, Internet and Mobile Phones) in which the advertiser pays an advertising agency to place the ad
- Below the line _____: All other _____. Much of this is intended to be subtle enough for the consumer to be unaware that _____ is taking place. E.g. sponsorship, product placement, endorsements, sales _____, merchandising, direct mail, personal selling, public relations, trade shows

a. Technology maturity lifecycle  
c. M80  
b. Cash and carry  
d. Promotion

12. _____s is the social science that studies the production, distribution, and consumption of goods and services. The term _____s comes from the Ancient Greek oá¼°κονομῖα from oá¼¶κος (oikos, 'house') + vÏŒμος (nomos, 'custom' or 'law'), hence 'rules of the house(hold)'. Current _____ models developed out of the broader field of political economy in the late 19th century, owing to a desire to use an empirical approach more akin to the physical sciences.

a. Economic  
c. ADTECH  
b. Industrial organization  
d. ACNielsen

13. _____ was originally coined by Austrian psychologist Alfred Adler in 1929. The current broader sense of the word dates from 1961.

In sociology, a _____ is the way a person lives.

a. 6-3-5 Brainwriting  
c. 180SearchAssistant  
b. Power III  
d. Lifestyle

14. A personal and cultural _____ is a relative ethic _____, an assumption upon which implementation can be extrapolated. A _____ system is a set of consistent _____s and measures that is soo not true. A principle _____ is a foundation upon which other _____s and measures of integrity are based.

a. Dolly Dimples  
c. Private branding  
b. Customization  
d. Value

15. _____ is the set of reasons that determines one to engage in a particular behavior. The term is generally used for human _____ but, theoretically, it can be used to describe the causes for animal behavior as well

a. Power III  
c. 180SearchAssistant  
b. Role playing  
d. Motivation

16. A _____ is a collection of symbols, experiences and associations connected with a product, a service, a person or any other artifact or entity.

_____s have become increasingly important components of culture and the economy, now being described as 'cultural accessories and personal philosophies'.

Some people distinguish the psychological aspect of a _____ from the experiential aspect.

a. Lovemarks  
b. Brand  
c. Status brand  
d. Naming rights

17. _____ or self identity refers to the global understanding a sentient being has of him or herself. It presupposes but can be distinguished from self-consciousness, which is simply an awareness of one's self. It is also more general than self-esteem, which is the purely evaluative element of the _____.

a. Need for cognition  
b. 180SearchAssistant  
c. Self-concept  
d. Power III

18. In psychology, philosophy, and the cognitive sciences, _____ is the process of attaining awareness or understanding of sensory information. It is a task far more complex than was imagined in the 1950s and 1960s, when it was predicted that building perceiving machines would take about a decade, a goal which is still very far from fruition. The word _____ comes from the Latin words _____, percepio, meaning 'receiving, collecting, action of taking possession, apprehension with the mind or senses.'

_____ is one of the oldest fields in psychology.

a. Power III  
b. 180SearchAssistant  
c. Groupthink  
d. Perception

19. _____ is a term that refers to the tendency of people to interpret information in a way that will support what they already believe. This concept, along with selective attention and selective retention, makes it hard for marketers to get their message across and create good product perception.

a. 180SearchAssistant  
b. Psychological Abstracts  
c. Selective distortion  
d. Power III

20. _____ is the process when people remember messages that are closer to their interests, values and beliefs more accurately, than those that are in contrast with their values and beliefs, selecting what to keep in the memory, narrowing the informational flow.

Such examples could include:

- A person may gradually reflect more positively on their time at school as they grow older
- A consumer might remember only the positive health benefits of a product they enjoy
- People tending to omit problems and disputes in past relationships
- A conspiracy theorist paying less attention to facts which do not aid their standpoint

a. 180SearchAssistant  
b. Power III  
c. Selective retention  
d. 6-3-5 Brainwriting

## Chapter 5. Consumer and Business Buyer Behavior

21. _____ is a form of communication that typically attempts to persuade potential customers to purchase or to consume more of a particular brand of product or service. 'While now central to the contemporary global economy and the reproduction of global production networks, it is only quite recently that _____ has been more than a marginal influence on patterns of sales and production. The formation of modern _____ was intimately bound up with the emergence of new forms of monopoly capitalism around the end of the 19th and beginning of the 20th century as one element in corporate strategies to create, organize and where possible control markets, especially for mass produced consumer goods.

   a. ACNielsen
   b. Advertising
   c. AMAX
   d. ADTECH

22. _____? is an American advertising campaign encouraging the consumption of cow's milk, which was created by the advertising agency Goodby Silverstein ' Partners for the California Milk Processor Board in 1993 and later licensed for use by milk processors and dairy farmers. It has been running since October 1993. The campaign has been credited with greatly increasing milk sales nationwide after a 20-year slump.

   a. Just Say No
   b. For Your Consideration
   c. You Got the Right One, Baby
   d. Got Milk?

23. In economics, an externality or spillover of an economic transaction is an impact on a party that is not directly involved in the transaction. In such a case, prices do not reflect the full costs or benefits in production or consumption of a product or service. A positive impact is called an _____ benefit, while a negative impact is called an _____ cost.

   a. External
   b. ACNielsen
   c. AMAX
   d. ADTECH

24. _____ is systematic determination of merit, worth, and significance of something or someone using criteria against a set of standards. _____ often is used to characterize and appraise subjects of interest in a wide range of human enterprises, including the arts, criminal justice, foundations and non-profit organizations, government, health care, and other human services.

Depending on the topic of interest, there are professional groups which look to the quality and rigor of the _____ process.

   a. ADTECH
   b. AMAX
   c. ACNielsen
   d. Evaluation

25. Cognition is the scientific term for 'the process of thought.' Its usage varies in different ways in accord with different disciplines: For example, in psychology and _____ science it refers to an information processing view of an individual's psychological functions. Other interpretations of the meaning of cognition link it to the development of concepts; individual minds, groups, organizations, and even larger coalitions of entities, can be modelled as 'societies' (Society of Mind), which cooperate to form concepts.

The autonomous elements of each 'society' would have the opportunity to demonstrate emergent behavior in the face of some crisis or opportunity.

   a. 6-3-5 Brainwriting
   b. 180SearchAssistant
   c. Power III
   d. Cognitive

## Chapter 5. Consumer and Business Buyer Behavior

26. _____ is an uncomfortable feeling caused by holding two contradictory ideas simultaneously. The 'ideas' or 'cognitions' in question may include attitudes and beliefs, and also the awareness of one's behavior. The theory of _____ proposes that people have a motivational drive to reduce dissonance by changing their attitudes, beliefs, and behaviors, or by justifying or rationalizing their attitudes, beliefs, and behaviors.
   a. 180SearchAssistant
   b. Perception
   c. Power III
   d. Cognitive dissonance

27. _____, a business term, is a measure of how products and services supplied by a company meet or surpass customer expectation. It is seen as a key performance indicator within business and is part of the four perspectives of a Balanced Scorecard.

In a competitive marketplace where businesses compete for customers, _____ is seen as a key differentiator and increasingly has become a key element of business strategy.

   a. Psychological pricing
   b. Street date
   c. Safety stock
   d. Customer satisfaction

28. _____ is a fee paid on borrowed assets. It is the price paid for the use of borrowed money, or, money earned by deposited funds. Assets that are sometimes lent with _____ include money, shares, consumer goods through hire purchase, major assets such as aircraft, and even entire factories in finance lease arrangements.
   a. ACNielsen
   b. ADTECH
   c. AMAX
   d. Interest

29. _____, an invented personal and cultural icon, is a brand name and trademark of American Fortune 500 corporation General Mills. The name was first developed by the Washburn Crosby Company in 1921 as a way to give a personalized response to consumer product questions. The name Betty was selected because it was viewed as a cheery, All-American name.
   a. Morris the Cat
   b. Power III
   c. Betty Crocker
   d. 180SearchAssistant

30. The Oxford University Press defines _____ as 'marketing on a worldwide scale reconciling or taking commercial advantage of global operational differences, similarities and opportunities in order to meet global objectives.' Oxford University Press' Glossary of Marketing Terms.

Here are three reasons for the shift from domestic to _____ as given by the authors of the textbook, _____ Management--3rd Edition by Masaaki Kotabe and Kristiaan Helsen, 2004.

One of the product categories in which global competition has been easy to track is in U.S. automotive sales.

   a. Guerrilla Marketing
   b. Global marketing
   c. Cause-related Marketing
   d. Relationship marketing

31. _____ is a term commonly used to describe commerce transactions between businesses like the one between a manufacturer and a wholesaler or a wholesaler and a retailer i.e both the buyer and the seller are business entity. This is unlike business-to-consumers (B2C) which involve a business entity and end consumer, or business-to-government (B2G) which involve a business entity and government.

The volume of B2B transactions is much higher than the volume of B2C transactions. The primary reason for this is that in a typical supply chain there will be many B2B transactions involving subcomponent or raw materials, and only one B2C transaction, specifically sale of the finished product to the end customer.

a. Business-to-business
b. Disruptive technology
c. Customer analytics
d. Cannibalization

32. In economics, _____ is the desire to own something and the ability to pay for it. The term _____ signifies the ability or the willingness to buy a particular commodity at a given point of time .

a. Discretionary spending
b. Market dominance
c. Market system
d. Demand

33. _____ is a term in economics, where demand for one good or service occurs as a result of demand for another. This may occur as the former is a part of production of the second. For example, demand for coal leads to _____ for mining, as coal must be mined for coal to be consumed.

a. 180SearchAssistant
b. 6-3-5 Brainwriting
c. Power III
d. Derived demand

34. In economics, _____ describes the state of a market with respect to competition.

- Perfect competition, in which the market consists of a very large number of firms producing a homogeneous product.
- Monopolistic competition where there are a large number of independent firms which have a very small proportion of the market share.
- Oligopoly, in which a market is dominated by a small number of firms which own more than 40% of the market share.
- Oligopsony, a market dominated by many sellers and a few buyers.
- Monopoly, where there is only one provider of a product or service.
- Natural monopoly, a monopoly in which economies of scale cause efficiency to increase continuously with the size of the firm. A firm is a natural monopoly if it is able to serve the entire market demand at a lower cost than any combination of two or more smaller, more specialized firms.
- Monopsony, when there is only one buyer in a market.

The imperfectly competitive structure is quite identical to the realistic market conditions where some monopolistic competitors, monopolists, oligopolists, and duopolists exist and dominate the market conditions. The elements of _____ include the number and size distribution of firms, entry conditions, and the extent of differentiation.

a. Money
b. Market structure
c. Law of supply
d. Perfect competition

35. A _____, in marketing, procurement, and organizational studies, is a group of employees, family members, or members of any type of organization responsible for purchasing an item for the organization. In a business setting, major purchases typically require input from various parts of the organization, including finance, accounting, purchasing, information technology management, and senior management. Highly technical purchases, such as information systems or production equipment, also require the expertise of technical specialists.

a. Customer Interaction Tracker
c. Customer insight

b. Technology acceptance model
d. Buying center

36. A supply chain is the system of organizations, people, technology, activities, information and resources involved in moving a product or service from _____ to customer. Supply chain activities transform natural resources, raw materials and components into a finished product that is delivered to the end customer. In sophisticated supply chain systems, used products may re-enter the supply chain at any point where residual value is recyclable.

a. Supplier
c. Relationship Management Application

b. Little value placed on potential benefits
d. GE matrix

37. _____ is a systematic method to improve the 'value' of goods or products and services by using an examination of function. Value, as defined, is the ratio of function to cost. Value can therefore be increased by either improving the function or reducing the cost.

a. 180SearchAssistant
c. Power III

b. Productivity
d. Value engineering

38. A _____ is an explicit set of requirements to be satisfied by a material, product, or service.

In engineering, manufacturing, and business, it is vital for suppliers, purchasers, and users of materials, products, or services to understand and agree upon all requirements. A _____ is a type of a standard which is often referenced by a contract or procurement document.

a. New product screening
c. Specification tree

b. Product development
d. Specification

39. _____ is the business-to-business or business-to-consumer or Business-to-government purchase and sale of supplies, Work and services through the Internet as well as other information and networking systems, such as Electronic Data Interchange and Enterprise Resource Planning. Typically, _____ Web sites allow qualified and registered users to look for buyers or sellers of goods and services. Depending on the approach, buyers or sellers may specify costs or invite bids.

a. ADTECH
c. E-procurement

b. AMAX
d. ACNielsen

40. _____ is a family of business models in which the buyer of a product provides certain information to a supplier of that product and the supplier takes full responsibility for maintaining an agreed inventory of the material, usually at the buyer's consumption location (usually a store.) A third party logistics provider can also be involved to make sure that the buyer have the required level of inventory by adjusting the demand and supply gaps.

As a symbiotic relationship, _____ makes it less likely that a business will unintentionally become out of stock of a good and reduces inventory in the supply chain.

a. Merchandise management system
c. Fulfillment house
b. Customer driven supply chain
d. Vendor Managed Inventory

41. _____ is a list for goods and materials held available in stock by a business. It is also used for a list of the contents of a household and for a list for testamentary purposes of the possessions of someone who has died. In accounting _____ is considered an asset.
   a. Ending Inventory
   c. Inventory
   b. ACNielsen
   d. ADTECH

42. _____ refers to a business or organization attempting to acquire goods or services to accomplish the goals of the enterprise. Though there are several organizations that attempt to set standards in the _____ process, processes can vary greatly between organizations. Typically the word '_____' is not used interchangeably with the word 'procurement', since procurement typically includes Expediting, Supplier Quality, and Traffic and Logistics (T'L) in addition to _____.
   a. Drop shipping
   c. Slip sheet
   b. Supply chain network
   d. Purchasing

## Chapter 6. Segmentation, Targeting, and Positioning

1. The Program (or Project) Evaluation and Review Technique, commonly abbreviated _____, is a model for project management designed to analyze and represent the tasks involved in completing a given project.

   _____ is a method to analyze the involved tasks in completing a given project, especially the time needed to complete each task, and identifying the minimum time needed to complete the total project.

   This model was invented by Booz Allen Hamilton, Inc.

   a. 6-3-5 Brainwriting
   b. 180SearchAssistant
   c. Power III
   d. Pert

2. Procter is a surname, and may also refer to:

   - Bryan Waller Procter (pseud. Barry Cornwall), English poet
   - Goodwin Procter, American law firm
   - _____, consumer products multinational

   a. Push
   b. Developed country
   c. Procter ' Gamble
   d. Comparison-Shopping agent

3. In the technical language of the World Trade Organization (WTO) system, a _____ is used to restrain international trade in order to protect a certain home industry from foreign competition. A member may take a '_____' action (i.e., restrict importation of a product temporarily) to protect a specific domestic industry from an increase in imports of any product which is causing, or which is threatening to cause, serious injury to the domestic industry that produces like or directly-competitive products.

   _____ measures were always available under the General Agreement on Tariffs and Trade (GATT) (Article XIX).

   a. Customs union
   b. Countervailing duties
   c. Gray market
   d. Safeguard

4. _____ is a broad label that refers to any individuals or households that use goods and services generated within the economy. The concept of a _____ is used in different contexts, so that the usage and significance of the term may vary.

   A _____ is a person who uses any product or service.

   a. 6-3-5 Brainwriting
   b. 180SearchAssistant
   c. Power III
   d. Consumer

5. _____ is the study of the Earth and its lands, features, inhabitants, and phenomena. A literal translation would be 'to describe or write about the Earth'. The first person to use the word '_____' was Eratosthenes.

   a. Geography
   b. Power III
   c. 6-3-5 Brainwriting
   d. 180SearchAssistant

## Chapter 6. Segmentation, Targeting, and Positioning

6. A _____ is a subgroup of people or organizations sharing one or more characteristics that cause them to have similar product and/or service needs. A true _____ meets all of the following criteria: it is distinct from other segments (different segments have different needs), it is homogeneous within the segment (exhibits common needs); it responds similarly to a market stimulus, and it can be reached by a market intervention. The term is also used when consumers with identical product and/or service needs are divided up into groups so they can be charged different amounts.
   a. Vertical market
   b. Law of disruption
   c. Societal marketing
   d. Market segment

7. In economics, a _____ exists when a specific individual or enterprise has sufficient control over a particular product or service to determine significantly the terms on which other individuals shall have access to it. Monopolies are thus characterized by a lack of economic competition for the good or service that they provide and a lack of viable substitute goods. The verb 'monopolize' refers to the process by which a firm gains persistently greater market share than what is expected under perfect competition.
   a. Monopoly
   b. Power III
   c. 6-3-5 Brainwriting
   d. 180SearchAssistant

8. In environmental modeling and especially in hydrology, a _____ model means a model that is acceptably consistent with observed natural processes, i.e. that simulates well, for example, observed river discharge. It is a key concept of the so-called Generalized Likelihood Uncertainty Estimation (GLUE) methodology to quantify how uncertain environmental predictions are.
   a. 180SearchAssistant
   b. 6-3-5 Brainwriting
   c. Power III
   d. Behavioral

9. _____ or _____ data refers to selected population characteristics as used in government, marketing or opinion research, or the _____ profiles used in such research. Note the distinction from the term 'demography' Commonly-used _____ include race, age, income, disabilities, mobility (in terms of travel time to work or number of vehicles available), educational attainment, home ownership, employment status, and even location.
   a. African Americans
   b. Demographic
   c. AStore
   d. Albert Einstein

10. In the field of marketing, demographics, opinion research, and social research in general, _____ variables are any attributes relating to personality, values, attitudes, interests, or lifestyles. They are also called IAO variables . They can be contrasted with demographic variables (such as age and gender), behavioral variables (such as usage rate or loyalty), and bizographic variables (such as industry, seniority and functional area.)
    a. Context analysis
    b. Product differentiation
    c. Customer Interaction Tracker
    d. Psychographic

11. Its a tool for marketing. _____ is a multivariate statistical classification technique for discovering whether the individuals of a population fall into different groups by making quantitative comparisons of multiple characteristics with the assumption that the differences within any group should be less than the differences between groups.

The information technologies employed in _____ include geographic information system and database management software.

## Chapter 6. Segmentation, Targeting, and Positioning

a. Linear discriminant analysis
b. Geodemographic segmentation
c. Discriminant analysis
d. Principal component analysis

12.

_____ was founded in 1986 by Laszlo Bardos, Andrew Dressel, John Haller, Mike Marvin, and Sean O'Sullivan. The company originated as a Rensselaer Polytechnic Institute (RPI) incubator project. The original name was Navigational Technologies Incorporated (NTI), and the first intended product was for in-car navigation.

a. MapInfo
b. Weber Shandwick
c. VideoJug
d. Partnership for a Drug-Free America

13. _____ is defined by the American _____ Association as the activity, set of institutions, and processes for creating, communicating, delivering, and exchanging offerings that have value for customers, clients, partners, and society at large. The term developed from the original meaning which referred literally to going to market, as in shopping, or going to a market to sell goods or services.

_____ practice tends to be seen as a creative industry, which includes advertising, distribution and selling.

a. Marketing
b. Product naming
c. Business marketing
d. Gatefold

14. _____ is a market coverage strategy in which a firm decides to ignore market segment differences and go after the whole market with one offer.it is type of marketing (or attempting to sell through persuasion) of a product to a wide audience. The idea is to broadcast a message that will reach the largest number of people possible. Traditionally _____ has focused on radio, television and newspapers as the medium used to reach this broad audience.

a. Business-to-consumer
b. Product naming
c. Value chain
d. Mass marketing

15. _____, in marketing, manufacturing, and management, is the use of flexible computer-aided manufacturing systems to produce custom output. Those systems combine the low unit costs of mass production processes with the flexibility of individual customization.

'_____' is the new frontier in business competition for both manufacturing and service industries.

a. Vertical integration
b. Flanking marketing warfare strategies
c. Power III
d. Mass customization

16. _____ is the practice of tailoring products, brands (microbrands), and promotions to meet the needs and wants of microsegments within a market. It is a type of market customization that deals with pricing of customer/product combinations at the store or individual level.

Standard pricing policy ignores the differences in customer segments of specific stores within a regional chain of stores.

## Chapter 6. Segmentation, Targeting, and Positioning

a. Reseller
b. Chief privacy officer
c. Value-based pricing
d. Micromarketing

17. _____ refers to marketing strategies applied directly to a specific consumer.

Having the knowledge on the consumer preferences, there are suggested personalized products and promotions to each consumer.

The _____ is based in four main steps in order to fulfill its goals: Those stages are identify, differentiate, interact, and customize.

a. AMAX
b. ACNielsen
c. One-to-one marketing
d. ADTECH

18. On an intranet or B2E Enterprise Web portals, personalization is often based on user attributes such as department, functional area, or role. The term _____ in this context refers to the ability of users to modify the page layout or specify what content should be displayed.

There are two categories of personalizations:

1. Rule-based
2. Content-based

Web personalization models include rules-based filtering, based on 'if this, then that' rules processing, and collaborative filtering, which serves relevant material to customers by combining their own personal preferences with the preferences of like-minded others. Collaborative filtering works well for books, music, video, etc.

a. Generic brands
b. Hawkers
c. Maturity of Organizations and Business Excellence - The Four-Phase Model
d. Customization

19. The _____ is an independent agency of the United States government, established in 1914 by the _____ Act. Its principal mission is the promotion of 'consumer protection' and the elimination and prevention of what regulators perceive to be harmfully 'anti-competitive' business practices, such as coercive monopoly.

The _____ Act was one of President Wilson's major acts against trusts.

a. Power III
b. 6-3-5 Brainwriting
c. 180SearchAssistant
d. Federal Trade Commission

20. A _____ is a process that can allow an organization to concentrate its limited resources on the greatest opportunities to increase sales and achieve a sustainable competitive advantage. A _____ should be centered around the key concept that customer satisfaction is the main goal.

## Chapter 6. Segmentation, Targeting, and Positioning

A _____ is most effective when it is an integral component of corporate strategy, defining how the organization will successfully engage customers, prospects, and competitors in the market arena.

a. Law of disruption  
c. Vertical market  
b. Marketspace  
d. Marketing strategy

21. Human beings are also considered to be _____ because they have the ability to change raw materials into valuable _____. The term Human _____ can also be defined as the skills, energies, talents, abilities and knowledge that are used for the production of goods or the rendering of services. While taking into account human beings as _____, the following things have to be kept in mind:

- The size of the population
- The capabilities of the individuals in that population

Many _____ cannot be consumed in their original form. They have to be processed in order to change them into more usable commodities.

a. 180SearchAssistant  
c. 6-3-5 Brainwriting  
b. Power III  
d. Resources

22. _____ is a form of communication that typically attempts to persuade potential customers to purchase or to consume more of a particular brand of product or service. 'While now central to the contemporary global economy and the reproduction of global production networks, it is only quite recently that _____ has been more than a marginal influence on patterns of sales and production. The formation of modern _____ was intimately bound up with the emergence of new forms of monopoly capitalism around the end of the 19th and beginning of the 20th century as one element in corporate strategies to create, organize and where possible control markets, especially for mass produced consumer goods.

a. AMAX  
c. ACNielsen  
b. ADTECH  
d. Advertising

23. Competitiveness is a comparative concept of the ability and performance of a firm, sub-sector or country to sell and supply goods and/or services in a given market. Although widely used in economics and business management, the usefulness of the concept, particularly in the context of national competitiveness, is vigorously disputed by economists, such as Paul Krugman .

The term may also be applied to markets, where it is used to refer to the extent to which the market structure may be regarded as perfectly _____.

a. Customs union  
c. Free trade zone  
b. Competitive  
d. Geographical pricing

24. _____ is, in very basic words, a position a firm occupies against its competitors.

According to Michael Porter, the three methods for creating a sustainable _____ are through:

## Chapter 6. Segmentation, Targeting, and Positioning

1. Cost leadership - Cost advantage occurs when a firm delivers the same services as its competitors but at a lower cost;

2.

a. Competitive advantage
c. Power III
b. 6-3-5 Brainwriting
d. 180SearchAssistant

25. In marketing, _____ has come to mean the process by which marketers try to create an image or identity in the minds of their target market for its product, brand, or organization. It is the 'relative competitive comparison' their product occupies in a given market as perceived by the target market.

Re-_____ involves changing the identity of a product, relative to the identity of competing products, in the collective minds of the target market.

a. Positioning
c. Per-inquiry advertising
b. LIFO
d. Sigg bottles

26. A _____ is a plan of action designed to achieve a particular goal.

_____ is different from tactics. In military terms, tactics is concerned with the conduct of an engagement while _____ is concerned with how different engagements are linked.

a. 6-3-5 Brainwriting
c. Power III
b. 180SearchAssistant
d. Strategy

27. In marketing, _____ is the process of distinguishing the differences of a product or offering from others, to make it more attractive to a particular target market. This involves differentiating it from competitors' products as well as one's own product offerings.

Differentiation is a source of competitive advantage.

a. Market share
c. Business marketing
b. Google Advertising Professional
d. Product differentiation

28. _____ is an advertisement in which a particular product specifically mentions a competitor by name for the express purpose of showing why the competitor is inferior to the product naming it.

This should not be confused with parody advertisements, where a fictional product is being advertised for the purpose of poking fun at the particular advertisement, nor should it be confused with the use of a coined brand name for the purpose of comparing the product without actually naming an actual competitor. ('Wikipedia tastes better and is less filling than the Encyclopedia Galactica.')

## Chapter 6. Segmentation, Targeting, and Positioning

In the 1980s, during what has been referred to as the cola wars, soft-drink manufacturer Pepsi ran a series of advertisements where people, caught on hidden camera, in a blind taste test, chose Pepsi over rival Coca-Cola.

a. Heavy-up  
b. GL-70  
c. Cost per conversion  
d. Comparative advertising

29. The _____ is a marketing concept that was first proposed as a theory to explain a pattern among successful advertising campaigns of the early 1940s. It states that such campaigns made unique propositions to the customer and that this convinced them to switch brands. The term was invented by Rosser Reeves of Ted Bates ' Company.

a. ACNielsen  
b. Unique selling proposition  
c. AMAX  
d. ADTECH

30. A personal and cultural _____ is a relative ethic _____, an assumption upon which implementation can be extrapolated. A _____ system is a set of consistent _____s and measures that is soo not true. A principle _____ is a foundation upon which other _____s and measures of integrity are based.

a. Dolly Dimples  
b. Customization  
c. Private branding  
d. Value

31. In the field of marketing, a customer _____ consists of the sum total of benefits which a vendor promises that a customer will receive in return for the customer's associated payment (or other value-transfer.)

Put simply, the _____ is what the customer gets for his money.

Accordingly, a customer can evaluate a company's value-proposition on two broad dimensions with multiple subsets:

1. relative performance: what the customer gets from the vendor relative to a competitor's offering;
2. price: which consists of the payment the customer makes to acquire the product or service; plus the access cost

The vendor-company's marketing and sales efforts offer a customer _____; the vendor-company's delivery and customer-service processes then fulfill that value-proposition.

A value-proposition can assist in a firm's marketing strategy, and may guide a business to target a particular market segment.

a. Law of disruption  
b. Value proposition  
c. Market environment  
d. Product differentiation

32. The _____ is an economic indicator that measures the satisfaction of consumers across the U.S. economy. It is produced by the National Quality Research Center (NQRC) at the University of Michigan in Ann Arbor, Michigan.

The _____ interviews about 80,000 Americans annually and asks about their satisfaction with the goods and services they have consumed.

a. American Customer Satisfaction Index
c. ACNielsen
b. ADTECH
d. AMAX

33. _____, a business term, is a measure of how products and services supplied by a company meet or surpass customer expectation. It is seen as a key performance indicator within business and is part of the four perspectives of a Balanced Scorecard.

In a competitive marketplace where businesses compete for customers, _____ is seen as a key differentiator and increasingly has become a key element of business strategy.

a. Customer Satisfaction
c. Safety stock
b. Psychological pricing
d. Street date

## Chapter 7. Product, Services, and Branding Strategy

1. _____ is an advertisement in which a particular product specifically mentions a competitor by name for the express purpose of showing why the competitor is inferior to the product naming it.

This should not be confused with parody advertisements, where a fictional product is being advertised for the purpose of poking fun at the particular advertisement, nor should it be confused with the use of a coined brand name for the purpose of comparing the product without actually naming an actual competitor. ('Wikipedia tastes better and is less filling than the Encyclopedia Galactica.')

In the 1980s, during what has been referred to as the cola wars, soft-drink manufacturer Pepsi ran a series of advertisements where people, caught on hidden camera, in a blind taste test, chose Pepsi over rival Coca-Cola.

   a. Comparative advertising                      b. GL-70
   c. Heavy-up                                        d. Cost per conversion

2. In marketing, a _____ is a generic product augmented by everything that is needed for the customer to have a compelling reason to buy. The generic product is what is usually shipped to the customer. The _____ typically augments the generic product with training and support, manuals, cables, additional software or hardware, installation instructions, professional services, etc.
   a. Product innovation                         b. Whole product
   c. Value-based pricing                         d. Shop fitting

3. _____ is a broad label that refers to any individuals or households that use goods and services generated within the economy. The concept of a _____ is used in different contexts, so that the usage and significance of the term may vary.

A _____ is a person who uses any product or service.

   a. 180SearchAssistant                     b. Power III
   c. 6-3-5 Brainwriting                        d. Consumer

4. _____ is anything that is intended to save time, energy or frustration. A _____ store at a petrol station, for example, sells items that have nothing to do with gasoline/petrol, but it saves the consumer from having to go to a grocery store. '_____' is a very relative term and its meaning tends to change over time.
   a. Multidimensional scaling              b. Consumer confidence
   c. Demographic profile                     d. Convenience

5. _____ is the examining of goods or services from retailers with the intent to purchase at that time. _____ is an activity of selection and/or purchase. In some contexts it is considered a leisure activity as well as an economic one.
   a. Hawkers                                      b. Shopping
   c. Khodebshchik                            d. Discount store

6. _____ is defined by the American _____ Association as the activity, set of institutions, and processes for creating, communicating, delivering, and exchanging offerings that have value for customers, clients, partners, and society at large. The term developed from the original meaning which referred literally to going to market, as in shopping, or going to a market to sell goods or services.

_____ practice tends to be seen as a creative industry, which includes advertising, distribution and selling.

a. Marketing
b. Product naming
c. Gatefold
d. Business marketing

7. A _____ refers to how a corporation is perceived. It is a generally accepted image of what a company 'stands for'. The creation of a _____ is an exercise in perception management.
   a. Mass marketing
   b. Value proposition
   c. Corporate image
   d. Pinstorm

8. A _____ is something that is acted upon or used by or by human labour or industry, for use as a building material to create some product or structure. Often the term is used to denote material that came from nature and is in an unprocessed or minimally processed state. Iron ore, logs, and crude oil, would be examples.
   a. Power III
   b. 6-3-5 Brainwriting
   c. Raw material
   d. 180SearchAssistant

9. _____ is a form of communication that typically attempts to persuade potential customers to purchase or to consume more of a particular brand of product or service. 'While now central to the contemporary global economy and the reproduction of global production networks, it is only quite recently that _____ has been more than a marginal influence on patterns of sales and production. The formation of modern _____ was intimately bound up with the emergence of new forms of monopoly capitalism around the end of the 19th and beginning of the 20th century as one element in corporate strategies to create, organize and where possible control markets, especially for mass produced consumer goods.
   a. AMAX
   b. Advertising
   c. ACNielsen
   d. ADTECH

10. _____ is the systematic application of marketing along with other concepts and techniques to achieve specific behavioral goals for a social good. _____ can be applied to promote, for example, merit goods, make the society avoid demerit goods and thus to promote that considers society's well being as a whole. This may include asking people not to smoke in public areas, for example, ask them to use seat belts, prompting to make them follow speed limits.
    a. Social Marketing
    b. Corporate capabilities package
    c. Corporate image
    d. Blind taste test

11. A _____ is a type of business entity in which partners (owners) share with each other the profits or losses of the business undertaking in which all have invested. _____s are often favored over corporations for taxation purposes, as the _____ structure does not generally incur a tax on profits before it is distributed to the partners (i.e. there is no dividend tax levied.) However, depending on the _____ structure and the jurisdiction in which it operates, owners of a _____ may be exposed to greater personal liability than they would as shareholders of a corporation.
    a. Screener
    b. Colour trademark
    c. Contributory negligence
    d. Partnership

12. _____ is a business management strategy aimed at embedding awareness of quality in all organizational processes. _____ has been widely used in manufacturing, education, call centers, government, and service industries, as well as NASA space and science programs.

When used together as a phrase, the three words in this expression have the following meanings:

- Total: Involving the entire organization, supply chain, and/or product life cycle
- Quality: With its usual definitions, with all its complexities
- Management: The system of managing with steps like Plan, Organize, Control, Lead, Staff, provisioning and organizing.

As defined by the International Organization for Standardization (ISO):

> '_____ is a management approach for an organization, centered on quality, based on the participation of all its members and aiming at long-term success through customer satisfaction, and benefits to all members of the organization and to society.' ISO 8402:1994

One major aim is to reduce variation from every process so that greater consistency of effort is obtained. (Royse, D., Thyer, B., Padgett D., ' Logan T., 2006)

In Japan, _____ comprises four process steps, namely:

1. Kaizen - Focuses on 'Continuous Process Improvement', to make processes visible, repeatable and measurable.
2. Atarimae Hinshitsu - The idea that 'things will work as they are supposed to'.
3. Kansei - Examining the way the user applies the product leads to improvement in the product itself.
4. Miryokuteki Hinshitsu - The idea that 'things should have an aesthetic quality' (for example, a pen will write in a way that is pleasing to the writer.)

_____ requires that the company maintain this quality standard in all aspects of its business. This requires ensuring that things are done right the first time and that defects and waste are eliminated from operations.

a. Power III
b. 180SearchAssistant
c. 6-3-5 Brainwriting
d. Total quality management

13. In descriptive statistics, the _____ is the length of the smallest interval which contains all the data. It is calculated by subtracting the smallest observation (sample minimum) from the greatest (sample maximum) and provides an indication of statistical dispersion.

It is measured in the same units as the data.

a. Surcharge
b. Range
c. Black PRies
d. Hospitality point of sales systems

## Chapter 7. Product, Services, and Branding Strategy

14. Procter is a surname, and may also refer to:

- Bryan Waller Procter (pseud. Barry Cornwall), English poet
- Goodwin Procter, American law firm
- _____, consumer products multinational

a. Push  
b. Developed country  
c. Comparison-Shopping agent  
d. Procter ' Gamble

15. A _____ is a collection of symbols, experiences and associations connected with a product, a service, a person or any other artifact or entity.

_____s have become increasingly important components of culture and the economy, now being described as 'cultural accessories and personal philosophies'.

Some people distinguish the psychological aspect of a _____ from the experiential aspect.

a. Status brand  
b. Naming rights  
c. Lovemarks  
d. Brand

16. The _____ is a US law that applies to labels on many consumer products. It requires the label to state:

- The identity of the product;
- The name and place of business of the manufacturer, packer, or distributor; and
- The net quantity of contents.

The contents statement must include both metric and U.S. customary units.

Passed under Lyndon B. Johnson in 1966, the law first took effect on July 1, 1967. The metric labeling requirement was added in 1992 and took effect on February 14, 1994.

a. Power III  
b. 180SearchAssistant  
c. 6-3-5 Brainwriting  
d. Fair Packaging and Labeling Act

17. The _____ is an independent agency of the United States government, established in 1914 by the _____ Act. Its principal mission is the promotion of 'consumer protection' and the elimination and prevention of what regulators perceive to be harmfully 'anti-competitive' business practices, such as coercive monopoly.

The _____ Act was one of President Wilson's major acts against trusts.

a. 6-3-5 Brainwriting  
b. Power III  
c. 180SearchAssistant  
d. Federal Trade Commission

## Chapter 7. Product, Services, and Branding Strategy

18. The _____ of 1914 (15 U.S.C §§ 41-58, as amended) established the Federal Trade Commission (FTC), a bipartisan body of five members appointed by the President of the United States for seven year terms. This Commission was authorized to issue Cease and Desist orders to large corporations to curb unfair trade practices. This Act also gave more flexibility to the US congress for judicial matters.

   a. Product liability
   b. Sound trademark
   c. Madrid system
   d. Federal Trade Commission Act

19. The U.S. _____ is an agency of the United States Department of Health and Human Services and is responsible for regulating and supervising the safety of foods, dietary supplements, drugs, vaccines, biological medical products, blood products, medical devices, radiation-emitting devices, veterinary products, and cosmetics. The FDA also enforces section 361 of the Public Health Service Act and the associated regulations, including sanitation requirements on interstate travel as well as specific rules for control of disease on products ranging from pet turtles to semen donations for assisted reproductive medicine techniques.

The FDA is an agency within the United States Department of Health and Human Services responsible for protecting and promoting the nation's public health.

   a. 180SearchAssistant
   b. 6-3-5 Brainwriting
   c. Power III
   d. Food and Drug Administration

20. _____ is one of the four Ps of the marketing mix. The other three aspects are product, promotion, and place. It is also a key variable in microeconomic price allocation theory.

   a. Transfer pricing
   b. Pricing
   c. Resale price maintenance
   d. Cost-plus pricing

21. _____ is a service provided by many retailers of various products, primarily electronics, that provides the end-user with a resource for information regarding the product, and help if the product should malfunction. _____ can be found in most manuals for products in the form of a phone number, website address, or physical location.

The Internet has allowed for a new form of _____ to develop.

   a. Product life cycle management
   b. Street date
   c. Time to market
   d. Product support

22. The _____ is an economic indicator that measures the satisfaction of consumers across the U.S. economy. It is produced by the National Quality Research Center (NQRC) at the University of Michigan in Ann Arbor, Michigan.

The _____ interviews about 80,000 Americans annually and asks about their satisfaction with the goods and services they have consumed.

   a. American Customer Satisfaction Index
   b. ADTECH
   c. ACNielsen
   d. AMAX

23. _____, a business term, is a measure of how products and services supplied by a company meet or surpass customer expectation. It is seen as a key performance indicator within business and is part of the four perspectives of a Balanced Scorecard.

## Chapter 7. Product, Services, and Branding Strategy

In a competitive marketplace where businesses compete for customers, _____ is seen as a key differentiator and increasingly has become a key element of business strategy.

a. Street date
b. Safety stock
c. Psychological pricing
d. Customer Satisfaction

24. There are many important decisions about product and service development and marketing. In the process of product development and marketing we should focus on strategic decisions about product attributes, product branding, product packaging, product labeling and product support services. But product strategy also calls for building a _____.

a. Product line
b. Prosumer
c. Demand generation
d. Context analysis

25. _____ is a term used by project managers and project management (PM) organizations to describe methods for analyzing and collectively managing a group of current or proposed projects based on numerous key characteristics. The fundamental objective of the _____ process is to determine the optimal mix and sequencing of proposed projects to best achieve the organization's overall goals - typically expressed in terms of hard economic measures, business strategy goals, or technical strategy goals - while honoring constraints imposed by management or external real-world factors. Typical attributes of projects being analyzed in a _____ process include each project's total expected cost, consumption of scarce resources (human or otherwise) expected timeline and schedule of investment, expected nature, magnitude and timing of benefits to be realized, and relationship or inter-dependencies with other projects in the portfolio.

a. Customer intelligence
b. Pop-up ads
c. Power III
d. Project Portfolio Management

26. _____ refers to the marketing effects or outcomes that accrue to a product with its brand name compared with those that would accrue if the same product did not have the brand name. And, at the root of these marketing effects is consumers' knowledge. In other words, consumers' knowledge about a brand makes manufacturers/advertisers respond differently or adopt appropriately adapt measures for the marketing of the brand.

a. Brand implementation
b. Trade Symbols
c. Brand management
d. Brand equity

27. In marketing, _____ has come to mean the process by which marketers try to create an image or identity in the minds of their target market for its product, brand, or organization. It is the 'relative competitive comparison' their product occupies in a given market as perceived by the target market.

Re-_____ involves changing the identity of a product, relative to the identity of competing products, in the collective minds of the target market.

a. Sigg bottles
b. LIFO
c. Per-inquiry advertising
d. Positioning

28.

The net present value (NPV) of all of a company's customers in terms of customer loyalty and indirectly, the revenue that the company can obtain from them.

## Chapter 7. Product, Services, and Branding Strategy

In deciding the value of a company, it is important to know of how much value its customer base is in terms of future revenues. The greater the _____ , the more future revenue in the lifetime of its clients; this means that a company with a higher _____ can get more money from its customers on average than another company that is identical in all other characteristics.

a. Marginal revenue  
b. Household production function  
c. Customer equity  
d. Hoarding

29. _____ is when a large distribution channel member (usually a retailer), buys from a manufacturer in bulk and puts its own name on the product. This strategy is only practical when the retailer does very high levels of volume. The advantages to the retailer are:

- more freedom and flexibility in pricing
- more control over product attributes and quality
- higher margins (or lower selling price)
- eliminates much of the manufacturer's promotional costs

The advantages to the manufacturer are:

- reduced promotional costs
- stability of sales volume (at least while the contract is operative)

- Kumar, Nirmalya; Steenkamp, Jan-Benedict E.M., Private Label Strategy - How to Meet the Store Brand Challenge. Harvard Business Press 2007

- private label
- brand management
- brand
- product management
- marketing

a. Clutter  
b. Private branding  
c. Black PRies  
d. Motion Picture Association of America's film-rating system

30. _____s (house brands in the United States, own brands in the UK, and home brands in Australia) are brands which are specific to a retail store or store chain. The retailer can manufacture goods under its own label, re-brand private label goods, or outsource manufacture of _____ items to multiple third parties - often the same manufacturers that produce brand label goods. _____ goods are generally cheaper than national brand goods because the retailer can optimize the production to suit consumer demand and reduce advertising costs.

a. Brand licensing  
b. Visual merchandising  
c. Channel conflict  
d. Store brand

## Chapter 7. Product, Services, and Branding Strategy

31. The verb _____ or grant _____ means to give permission. The noun _____ refers to that permission as well as to the document memorializing that permission. _____ may be granted by a party to another party as an element of an agreement between those parties.

a. License
c. 6-3-5 Brainwriting

b. 180SearchAssistant
d. Power III

32. A _____ is the price one pays as remuneration for services, especially the honorarium paid to a doctor, lawyer, consultant, or other member of a learned profession. _____s usually allow for overhead, wages, costs, and markup.

Traditionally, professionals in Great Britain received a _____ in contradistinction to a payment, salary, or wage, and would often use guineas rather than pounds as units of account.

a. Price maintenance
c. Price

b. Fee
d. Price points

33. A product _____ is the use of an established product's brand name for a new item in the same product category. _____s occur when a company introduces additional items in the same product category under the same brand name such as new flavors, forms, colors, added ingredients, package sizes. Examples includei) Zen LXI, Zen VXIii) Surf, Surf Excel, Surf Excel Blueiii) Splendour, Splendour Plusiv) Coke, Diet Coke, Vanilla Cokev) Clinic All Clear, Clinic Plus

- brand
- brand management
- marketing
- product management
- Product lining

a. Cross merchandising
c. Brand parity

b. National brand
d. Line extension

34. A _____ is the use of an established product's brand name for a new item in the same product category. _____s occur when a company introduces additional items in the same product category under the same brand name such as new flavors, forms, colors, added ingredients, package sizes.

a. Positioning
c. Flighting

b. Lifestyles of Health and Sustainability
d. Product line extension

35. _____ or brand stretching is a marketing strategy in which a firm marketing a product with a well-developed image uses the same brand name in a different product category. Organizations use this strategy to increase and leverage brand equity (definition: the net worth and long-term sustainability just from the renowned name.) An example of a _____ is Jello-gelatin creating Jello pudding pops.

a. Trade Symbols
c. Visual merchandising

b. Web 2.0
d. Brand extension

36. _____ is used in marketing to describe the inability to assess the value gained from engaging in an activity using any tangible evidence. It is often used to describe services where there isn't a tangible product that the customer can purchase, that can be seen, tasted or touched.

Other key characteristics of services include perishability, inseparability and variability.

a. Inseparability
b. Intangibility
c. Individual branding
d. Automated surveys

37. _____ is used in marketing to describe a key quality of services as distinct from goods. _____ is the characteristic that a service has which renders it impossible to divorce the supply or production of the service from its consumption.

Other key characteristics of services include perishability, intangibility and variability.

a. Individual branding
b. Engagement
c. Online focus group
d. Inseparability

38. _____ is used in marketing to describe the way in which service capacity cannot be stored for sale in the future. It is a key concept of services marketing.

Other key characteristics of services include intangibility, inseparability and variability.

a. Target audience
b. Specialty catalogs
c. Customerization
d. Perishability

39. _____ is a measure of the strength of a brand, product, service relative to competitive offerings. There is often a geographic element to the competitive landscape. In defining _____, you must see to what extent a product, brand, or firm controls a product category in a given geographic area.

a. Market system
b. Discretionary spending
c. Market dominance
d. Productivity

40. In statistics, an _____ is a term in a statistical model added when the effect of two or more variables is not simply additive. Such a term reflects that the effect of one variable depends on the values of one or more other variables.

Thus, for a response Y and two variables $x_1$ and $x_2$ an additive model would be:

$$Y = ax_1 + bx_2 + \text{error}$$

In contrast to this,

$$Y = ax_1 + bx_2 + c(x_1 \times x_2) + \text{error},$$

is an example of a model with an _____ between variables $x_1$ and $x_2$ ('error' refers to the random variable whose value by which y differs from the expected value of y.)

## Chapter 7. Product, Services, and Branding Strategy

a. ADTECH
c. ACNielsen
b. Interaction
d. AMAX

41. A _____ is a process that can allow an organization to concentrate its limited resources on the greatest opportunities to increase sales and achieve a sustainable competitive advantage. A _____ should be centered around the key concept that customer satisfaction is the main goal.

A _____ is most effective when it is an integral component of corporate strategy, defining how the organization will successfully engage customers, prospects, and competitors in the market arena.

a. Law of disruption
c. Marketing strategy
b. Vertical market
d. Marketspace

42. The _____ establishes relationships among profitablity, customer loyalty, and employee satisfaction, loyalty, and productivity. The links in the chain (which should be regarded as propositions) as follows: Profit and growth are stimulated primarily by customer loyalty. Loyalty is a direct result of customer satisfaction.
a. Chief privacy officer
c. Discontinuation
b. Micromarketing
d. Service-profit chain

43. _____ is an ongoing process that occurs strictly within a company or organization whereby the functional process aligns, motivates and empowers employees at all management levels to consistently deliver a satisfying customer experience. According to Burkitt and Zealley, 'the challenge for _____ is not only to get the right messages across, but to embed them in such a way that they both change and reinforce employee behaviour'.
a. Internal marketing
c. AMAX
b. ACNielsen
d. ADTECH

44. _____ refers to the evolving trend in marketing whereby marketing has moved from a transaction-based effort to a conversation. The definition of _____ comes from John Deighton at Harvard, who says _____ is the ability to address the customer, remember what the customer says and address the customer again in a way that illustrates that we remember what the customer has told us (Deighton 1996.) _____ is not synonymous with online marketing, although _____ processes are facilitated by internet technology.
a. European Information Technology Observatory
c. Outsourcing relationship management
b. Interactive marketing
d. InfoNU

45. _____ in economics refers to metrics and measures of output from production processes, per unit of input. Labor _____, for example, is typically measured as a ratio of output per labor-hour, an input. _____ may be conceived of as a metrics of the technical or engineering efficiency of production.
a. Value engineering
c. 180SearchAssistant
b. Power III
d. Productivity

46. The _____ was enacted in 1972 by the United States Congress. It established the United States Consumer Product Safety Commission as an independent agency of the United States federal government and defined its basic authority. The act gives CPSC the power to develop safety standards and pursue recalls for products that present unreasonable or substantial risks of injury or death to consumers.

## Chapter 7. Product, Services, and Branding Strategy

a. 6-3-5 Brainwriting
c. Power III
b. 180SearchAssistant
d. Consumer Product Safety Act

47. The United States _____ is an independent agency of the United States government created in 1972 through the Consumer Product Safety Act to protect 'against unreasonable risks of injuries associated with consumer products.' As of 2006 its acting chairman is Nancy Nord, a Republican. The other commissioner is Thomas Hill Moore, a Democrat. Normally the board has three commissioners.
   a. Consumer Product Safety Commission
   c. 6-3-5 Brainwriting
   b. Power III
   d. 180SearchAssistant

48. The United States _____ to oversee the safety of food, drugs, and cosmetics. A principal author of this law was Royal S. Copeland, a three-term U.S. Senator from New York. In 1968, the Electronic Product Radiation Control provisions were added to the FD'C.
   a. Celler-Kefauver Act
   c. Trademark classification
   b. Product liability
   d. Federal Food, Drug, and Cosmetic Act

49. The Oxford University Press defines _____ as 'marketing on a worldwide scale reconciling or taking commercial advantage of global operational differences, similarities and opportunities in order to meet global objectives.' Oxford University Press' Glossary of Marketing Terms.

Here are three reasons for the shift from domestic to _____ as given by the authors of the textbook, _____ Management--3rd Edition by Masaaki Kotabe and Kristiaan Helsen, 2004.

One of the product categories in which global competition has been easy to track is in U.S. automotive sales.

   a. Relationship marketing
   c. Cause-related Marketing
   b. Guerrilla Marketing
   d. Global marketing

50. The _____ is a United States federal law (15 U.S.C. § 2301 et seq.). Enacted in 1975, it is the federal statute that governs warranties on consumer products.

The statute is remedial in nature and is intended to protect consumers from deceptive warranty practices. Consumer products are not required to have warranties, but if one is given, it must comply with the _____.

   a. Privacy law
   c. Patent
   b. Foreign Corrupt Practices Act
   d. Magnuson-Moss Warranty Act

51. _____ is marketing based on relationship and value. It may be used to market a service or a product.

Marketing a service-base business is different from marketing a goods-base business.

   a. 180SearchAssistant
   c. Power III
   b. 6-3-5 Brainwriting
   d. Services marketing

## Chapter 8. New-Product Development and Product Life-Cycle Strategies

1. _____ is the set of tasks, knowledge, and techniques required to identify business needs and determine solutions to business problems. Solutions often include a systems development component, but may also consist of process improvement or organizational change. The person who carries out this task is called a business analyst or _____.
   a. Performance-based advertising
   b. Door-to-door
   c. Business analysis
   d. Business structure

2. _____ is one of the four elements of marketing mix. An organization or set of organizations (go-betweens) involved in the process of making a product or service available for use or consumption by a consumer or business user.

   The other three parts of the marketing mix are product, pricing, and promotion.

   a. Clustering
   b. Distribution
   c. Better Living Through Chemistry
   d. LIFO

3. In economics, an externality or spillover of an economic transaction is an impact on a party that is not directly involved in the transaction. In such a case, prices do not reflect the full costs or benefits in production or consumption of a product or service. A positive impact is called an _____ benefit, while a negative impact is called an _____ cost.
   a. AMAX
   b. External
   c. ACNielsen
   d. ADTECH

4. A supply chain is the system of organizations, people, technology, activities, information and resources involved in moving a product or service from _____ to customer. Supply chain activities transform natural resources, raw materials and components into a finished product that is delivered to the end customer. In sophisticated supply chain systems, used products may re-enter the supply chain at any point where residual value is recyclable.
   a. GE matrix
   b. Supplier
   c. Little value placed on potential benefits
   d. Relationship Management Application

5. _____ is the process of using quantitative methods and qualitative methods to evaluate consumer response to a product idea prior to the introduction of a product to the market. It can also be used to generate communication designed to alter consumer attitudes toward existing products. These methods involve the evaluation by consumers of product concepts having certain rational benefits, such as 'a detergent that removes stains but is gentle on fabrics,' or non-rational benefits, such as 'a shampoo that lets you be yourself.' Such methods are commonly referred to as _____ and have been performed using field surveys, personal interviews and focus groups, in combination with various quantitative methods, to generate and evaluate product concepts.
   a. Concept testing
   b. Market analysis
   c. Marketing research process
   d. Cross tabulation

6. _____ is defined by the American _____ Association as the activity, set of institutions, and processes for creating, communicating, delivering, and exchanging offerings that have value for customers, clients, partners, and society at large. The term developed from the original meaning which referred literally to going to market, as in shopping, or going to a market to sell goods or services.

   _____ practice tends to be seen as a creative industry, which includes advertising, distribution and selling.

   a. Gatefold
   b. Product naming
   c. Business marketing
   d. Marketing

## Chapter 8. New-Product Development and Product Life-Cycle Strategies

7. In business and engineering, new _____ is the term used to describe the complete process of bringing a new product or service to market. There are two parallel paths involved in the Nproduct development process: one involves the idea generation, product design, and detail engineering; the other involves market research and marketing analysis. Companies typically see new _____ as the first stage in generating and commercializing new products within the overall strategic process of product life cycle management used to maintain or grow their market share.

   a. New product development  
   b. Product development  
   c. New product screening  
   d. Product optimization

8. A _____, in the field of business and marketing, is a geographic region or demographic group used to gauge the viability of a product or service in the mass market prior to a wide scale roll-out. The criteria used to judge the acceptability of a _____ region or group include:

   1. a population that is demographically similar to the proposed target market; and
   2. relative isolation from densely populated media markets so that advertising to the test audience can be efficient and economical.

The _____ ideally aims to duplicate 'everything' - promotion and distribution as well as `product' - on a smaller scale. The technique replicates, typically in one area, what is planned to occur in a national launch; and the results are very carefully monitored, so that they can be extrapolated to projected national results. The `area' may be any one of the following:

- Television area
- Test town
- Residential neighborhood
- Test site

A number of decisions have to be taken about any _____:

- Which _____?
- What is to be tested?
- How long a test?
- What are the success criteria?

The simple go or no-go decision, together with the related reduction of risk, is normally the main justification for the expense of _____s. At the same time, however, such _____s can be used to test specific elements of a new product's marketing mix; possibly the version of the product itself, the promotional message and media spend, the distribution channels and the price.

   a. Power III  
   b. Preadolescence  
   c. 180SearchAssistant  
   d. Test market

9. _____ is the process or cycle of introducing a new product into the market. The actual launch of a new product is the final stage of new product development, and the one where the most money will have to be spent for advertising, sales promotion, and other marketing efforts. In the case of a new consumer packaged good, costs will be at least $ 10 million, but can reach up to $ 200 million.

## Chapter 8. New-Product Development and Product Life-Cycle Strategies

a. Commercialization
b. Relationship management
c. Perceptual mapping
d. Value chain

10. Procter is a surname, and may also refer to:

- Bryan Waller Procter (pseud. Barry Cornwall), English poet
- Goodwin Procter, American law firm
- _____, consumer products multinational

a. Push
b. Developed country
c. Comparison-Shopping agent
d. Procter ' Gamble

11. _____ Management is the succession of strategies used by management as a product goes through its _____. The conditions in which a product is sold changes over time and must be managed as it moves through its succession of stages.

The _____ goes through many phases, involves many professional disciplines, and requires many skills, tools and processes.

a. Product life cycle
b. Small business
c. Safety stock
d. Business stature

12. A craze is a product, idea, cultural movement, or model that gains popularity among a small section of the populace then quickly migrates to the mainstream. Crazes are characterized by their lightning fast adoption and swift departure from public awareness. Crazes and _____s are also characterized by their unusually high interest and sales figures relative to the time they are active in the marketplace, as compared with other similar products, ideas, cultural movements or models.
a. Fad
b. 6-3-5 Brainwriting
c. Power III
d. 180SearchAssistant

13. _____ is a diversified financial services company with operations around the world. Wells Fargo is the fourth largest bank in the US by assets and the second largest bank by market cap.
a. Wells Fargo ' Co.
b. Point of sale
c. Green Earth Market
d. Westinghouse Electric

14. The _____ is generally accepted as the use and specification of the four p's describing the strategic position of a product in the marketplace. One version of the origins of the _____ starts in 1948 when James Culliton said that a marketing decision should be a result of something similar to a recipe. This version continued in 1953 when Neil Borden, in his American Marketing Association presidential address, took the recipe idea one step further and coined the term 'Marketing-Mix'.
a. Marketing mix
b. 180SearchAssistant
c. 6-3-5 Brainwriting
d. Power III

## Chapter 9. Pricing: Understanding and Capturing Customer Value

1. _____ in economics and business is the result of an exchange and from that trade we assign a numerical monetary value to a good, service or asset. If I trade 4 apples for an orange, the _____ of an orange is 4 - apples. Inversely, the _____ of an apple is 1/4 oranges.
   a. Transfer pricing
   b. Price
   c. Contribution margin-based pricing
   d. Price war

2. _____ is one of the four Ps of the marketing mix. The other three aspects are product, promotion, and place. It is also a key variable in microeconomic price allocation theory.
   a. Resale price maintenance
   b. Transfer pricing
   c. Cost-plus pricing
   d. Pricing

3. A personal and cultural _____ is a relative ethic _____, an assumption upon which implementation can be extrapolated. A _____ system is a set of consistent _____s and measures that is soo not true. A principle _____ is a foundation upon which other _____s and measures of integrity are based.
   a. Private branding
   b. Dolly Dimples
   c. Customization
   d. Value

4. In the field of marketing, a customer _____ consists of the sum total of benefits which a vendor promises that a customer will receive in return for the customer's associated payment (or other value-transfer.)

Put simply, the _____ is what the customer gets for his money.

Accordingly, a customer can evaluate a company's value-proposition on two broad dimensions with multiple subsets:

   1. relative performance: what the customer gets from the vendor relative to a competitor's offering;
   2. price: which consists of the payment the customer makes to acquire the product or service; plus the access cost

The vendor-company's marketing and sales efforts offer a customer _____; the vendor-company's delivery and customer-service processes then fulfill that value-proposition.

A value-proposition can assist in a firm's marketing strategy, and may guide a business to target a particular market segment.

   a. Law of disruption
   b. Product differentiation
   c. Market environment
   d. Value proposition

5. _____, or Value optimized pricing is a business strategy. It sets selling prices on the perceived value to the customer, rather than on the actual cost of the product, the market price, competitors prices, or the historical price.

The goal of _____ is to align price with value delivered.

   a. Product innovation
   b. Soft sell
   c. Mass market
   d. Value-based pricing

## Chapter 9. Pricing: Understanding and Capturing Customer Value

6. In psychology, philosophy, and the cognitive sciences, _____ is the process of attaining awareness or understanding of sensory information. It is a task far more complex than was imagined in the 1950s and 1960s, when it was predicted that building perceiving machines would take about a decade, a goal which is still very far from fruition. The word _____ comes from the Latin words _____, percepio, meaning 'receiving, collecting, action of taking possession, apprehension with the mind or senses.'

_____ is one of the oldest fields in psychology.

a. Groupthink
c. 180SearchAssistant

b. Power III
d. Perception

7. Procter is a surname, and may also refer to:

- Bryan Waller Procter (pseud. Barry Cornwall), English poet
- Goodwin Procter, American law firm
- _____, consumer products multinational

a. Push
c. Comparison-Shopping agent

b. Developed country
d. Procter ' Gamble

8. _____ refers to the additional value of a commodity over the cost of commodities used to produce it from the previous stage of production. An example is the price of gasoline at the pump over the price of the oil in it. In national accounts used in macroeconomics, it refers to the contribution of the factors of production, i.e., land, labor, and capital goods, to raising the value of a product and corresponds to the incomes received by the owners of these factors. The factors of production provide 'services' which raise the unit price of a product (X) relative to the cost per unit of intermediate goods used up in the production of X. _____ is shared between the factors of production (capital, labor, also human capital), giving rise to issues of distribution.

a. Consumer spending
c. Power III

b. Deregulation
d. Value added

9. In economics, business, retail, and accounting, a _____ is the value of money that has been used up to produce something, and hence is not available for use anymore. In economics, a _____ is an alternative that is given up as a result of a decision. In business, the _____ may be one of acquisition, in which case the amount of money expended to acquire it is counted as _____.

a. Cost
c. Marginal cost

b. Transaction cost
d. Fixed costs

10. In economics, _____ are business expenses that are not dependent on the activities of the business They tend to be time-related, such as salaries or rents being paid per month. This is in contrast to variable costs, which are volume-related (and are paid per quantity.)

In management accounting, _____ are defined as expenses that do not change in proportion to the activity of a business, within the relevant period or scale of production.

a. Marginal cost  
c. Variable cost  
b. Transaction cost  
d. Fixed costs  

11. _____s are used in open sentences. For instance, in the formula x + 1 = 5, x is a _____ which represents an 'unknown' number. _____s are often represented by letters of the Roman alphabet, or those of other alphabets, such as Greek, and use other special symbols.
   a. Quantitative
   b. Market specialization
   c. Sample sales
   d. Variable

12. _____s are expenses that change in proportion to the activity of a business. In other words, _____ is the sum of marginal costs. It can also be considered normal costs.
   a. Marginal cost
   b. Transaction cost
   c. Fixed costs
   d. Variable cost

13. _____ is a form of communication that typically attempts to persuade potential customers to purchase or to consume more of a particular brand of product or service. 'While now central to the contemporary global economy and the reproduction of global production networks, it is only quite recently that _____ has been more than a marginal influence on patterns of sales and production. The formation of modern _____ was intimately bound up with the emergence of new forms of monopoly capitalism around the end of the 19th and beginning of the 20th century as one element in corporate strategies to create, organize and where possible control markets, especially for mass produced consumer goods.
   a. Advertising
   b. ACNielsen
   c. ADTECH
   d. AMAX

14. _____ involves disseminating information about a product, product line, brand, or company. It is one of the four key aspects of the marketing mix. (The other three elements are product marketing, pricing, and distribution). P>_____ is generally sub-divided into two parts:

   - Above the line _____: Promotion in the media (e.g. TV, radio, newspapers, Internet and Mobile Phones) in which the advertiser pays an advertising agency to place the ad
   - Below the line _____: All other _____. Much of this is intended to be subtle enough for the consumer to be unaware that _____ is taking place. E.g. sponsorship, product placement, endorsements, sales _____, merchandising, direct mail, personal selling, public relations, trade shows

   a. Cash and carry
   b. Promotion
   c. Technology maturity lifecycle
   d. M80

15. _____ is a pricing method used by companies. It is used primarily because it is easy to calculate and requires little information. There are several varieties, but the common thread in all of them is that one first calculates the cost of the product, then includes an additional amount to represent profit.
   a. Relationship based pricing
   b. Cost-plus pricing
   c. Competitor indexing
   d. Price maintenance

## Chapter 9. Pricing: Understanding and Capturing Customer Value

16. In economics, and cost accounting, _____ describes the total economic cost of production and is made up of variable costs, which vary according to the quantity of a good produced and include inputs such as labor and raw materials, plus fixed costs, which are independent of the quantity of a good produced and include inputs (capital) that cannot be varied in the short term, such as buildings and machinery. _____ in economics includes the total opportunity cost of each factor of production in addition to fixed and variable costs.

The rate at which _____ changes as the amount produced changes is called marginal cost.

a. Hoarding
c. Marginal revenue

b. Household production function
d. Total cost

17. In economics, _____ is the desire to own something and the ability to pay for it. The term _____ signifies the ability or the willingness to buy a particular commodity at a given point of time.

a. Market dominance
c. Demand

b. Discretionary spending
d. Market system

18. _____ is a pricing method used by firms. It is defined as 'a cost management tool for reducing the overall cost of a product over its entire life-cycle with the help of production, engineering, research and design'. _____ finds the maximum amount of cost that can be incurred on a product and with it the firm can still earn the required profit margin from that product at a particular selling price.

a. Competitor indexing
c. Penetration pricing

b. Resale price maintenance
d. Target costing

19. _____ is a common market form. Many markets can be considered monopolistically competitive, often including the markets for restaurants, cereal, clothing, shoes and service industries in large cities. Short-run equilibrium of the firm under _____

Monopolistically competitive markets have the following characteristics:

- There are many producers and many consumers in a given market, and no business has total control over the market price.
- Consumers perceive that there are non-price differences among the competitors' products.
- There are few barriers to entry and exit.
- Producers have a degree of control over price.

Long-run equilibrium of the firm under _____

The characteristics of a monopolistically competitive market are almost the same as in perfect competition, with the exception of heterogeneous products, and that _____ involves a great deal of non-price competition (based on subtle product differentiation.) A firm making profits in the short run will break even in the long run because demand will decrease and average total cost will increase.

a. Law of supply  
b. Leading indicator  
c. Money  
d. Monopolistic competition

20. _____ is a rivalry between individuals, groups, nations for territory, a niche, or allocation of resources. It arises whenever two or more parties strive for a goal which cannot be shared. _____ occurs naturally between living organisms which co-exist in the same environment.

a. Price fixing  
b. Direct competition  
c. Non-price competition  
d. Competition

21. In economics, the _____ can be defined as the graph depicting the relationship between the price of a certain commodity, and the amount of it that consumers are willing and able to purchase at that given price. It is a graphic representation of a demand schedule The _____ for all consumers together follows from the _____ of every individual consumer: the individual demands at each price are added together.

_____s are used to estimate behaviors in competitive markets, and are often combined with supply curves to estimate the equilibrium price (the price at which sellers together are willing to sell the same amount as buyers together are willing to buy, also known as market clearing price) and the equilibrium quantity (the amount of that good or service that will be produced and bought without surplus/excess supply or shortage/excess demand) of that market.

a. Power III  
b. 180SearchAssistant  
c. 6-3-5 Brainwriting  
d. Demand curve

22. _____ is an advertisement in which a particular product specifically mentions a competitor by name for the express purpose of showing why the competitor is inferior to the product naming it.

This should not be confused with parody advertisements, where a fictional product is being advertised for the purpose of poking fun at the particular advertisement, nor should it be confused with the use of a coined brand name for the purpose of comparing the product without actually naming an actual competitor. ('Wikipedia tastes better and is less filling than the Encyclopedia Galactica.')

In the 1980s, during what has been referred to as the cola wars, soft-drink manufacturer Pepsi ran a series of advertisements where people, caught on hidden camera, in a blind taste test, chose Pepsi over rival Coca-Cola.

a. Cost per conversion  
b. Heavy-up  
c. GL-70  
d. Comparative advertising

23. In economics, a _____ exists when a specific individual or enterprise has sufficient control over a particular product or service to determine significantly the terms on which other individuals shall have access to it. Monopolies are thus characterized by a lack of economic competition for the good or service that they provide and a lack of viable substitute goods. The verb 'monopolize' refers to the process by which a firm gains persistently greater market share than what is expected under perfect competition.

a. 6-3-5 Brainwriting  
b. 180SearchAssistant  
c. Power III  
d. Monopoly

24. In economics, _____ describes demand that is not very sensitive to a change in price.

## Chapter 9. Pricing: Understanding and Capturing Customer Value

a. AMAX
b. ACNielsen
c. ADTECH
d. Inelastic

25. In economics, _____ is the ratio of the percent change in one variable to the percent change in another variable. It is a tool for measuring the responsiveness of a function to changes in parameters in a relative way. Commonly analyzed are _____ of substitution, price and wealth.
a. Elasticity
b. ACNielsen
c. Intellectual property
d. Opinion leadership

26. _____s is the social science that studies the production, distribution, and consumption of goods and services. The term _____s comes from the Ancient Greek οἰκονομῐ́α from οἶκος (oikos, 'house') + νόμος (nomos, 'custom' or 'law'), hence 'rules of the house(hold)'. Current _____ models developed out of the broader field of political economy in the late 19th century, owing to a desire to use an empirical approach more akin to the physical sciences.
a. Industrial organization
b. ACNielsen
c. ADTECH
d. Economic

27. A _____ is a company or individual that purchases goods or services with the intention of reselling them rather than consuming or using them. This is usually done for profit (but could be resold at a loss.) One example can be found in the industry of telecommunications, where companies buy excess amounts of transmission capacity or call time from other carriers and resell it to smaller carriers.
a. Micromarketing
b. Mass market
c. Reseller
d. Refusal to deal

28. _____ are prices at which demand is relatively high. In introductory microeconomics, a demand curve is downward sloping to the right and either linear or gently convex to the origin. The first is usually true, but the second is only piecewise true, as price surveys indicate that demand for a product is not a linear function of its price and not even a smooth function.
a. Pricing
b. Transfer pricing
c. Premium pricing
d. Price points

29. There are many important decisions about product and service development and marketing. In the process of product development and marketing we should focus on strategic decisions about product attributes, product branding, product packaging, product labeling and product support services. But product strategy also calls for building a _____.
a. Context analysis
b. Demand generation
c. Prosumer
d. Product line

30. A _____ is the price one pays as remuneration for services, especially the honorarium paid to a doctor, lawyer, consultant, or other member of a learned profession. _____s usually allow for overhead, wages, costs, and markup.

Traditionally, professionals in Great Britain received a _____ in contradistinction to a payment, salary, or wage, and would often use guineas rather than pounds as units of account.

a. Fee
b. Price
c. Price points
d. Price maintenance

# Chapter 9. Pricing: Understanding and Capturing Customer Value

31. _____ is a marketing strategy that involves offering several products for sale as one combined product. This strategy is very common in the software business (for example: bundle a word processor, a spreadsheet, and a database into a single office suite), in the cable television industry (for example, basic cable in the United States generally offers many channels at one price), and in the fast food industry in which multiple items are combined into a complete meal. A bundle of products is sometimes referred to as a package deal or a compilation or an anthology.
   a. Food marketing
   b. Multichannel marketing
   c. Product bundling
   d. Market segment

32. _____ is the process of understanding, anticipating and influencing consumer behavior in order to maximize revenue or profits from a fixed, perishable resource This process was first discovered by Dr. Matt H. Keller. The challenge is to sell the right resources to the right customer at the right time for the right price. This process can result in price discrimination, where a firm charges customers consuming otherwise identical goods or services a different price for doing so.
   a. Service provider
   b. Yield management
   c. Freebie marketing
   d. Multi-level marketing

33. _____ or price ending is a marketing practice based on the theory that certain prices have a psychological impact. The retail prices are often expressed as 'odd prices': a little less than a round number, e.g. $19.99 or £6.95 (but not necessarily mathematically odd, it could also be 2.98.) The theory is this drives demand greater than would be expected if consumers were perfectly rational.
   a. Small business
   b. Price-weighted
   c. Time to market
   d. Psychological pricing

34. A _____ or leader is a product sold at a low price (at cost or below cost) to stimulate other, profitable sales. It is a kind of sales promotion, in other words marketing concentrating on a pricing strategy. The price can even be so low that the product is sold at a loss.
   a. Loss leader
   b. Pricing
   c. Pricing objectives
   d. Price war

35. A _____ is an amount paid by way of reduction, return, or refund on what has already been paid or contributed. It is a type of sales promotion marketers use primarily as incentives or supplements to product sales. The mail-in _____ is the most common.
   a. Package-on-Package
   b. Market specialization
   c. Convergent
   d. Rebate

36. An _____ is quite usually a standard guarantee from the seller of a product that specifies the extent to which the quality or performance of the product is assured and states the conditions under which the product can be returned, replaced, or repaired. It is often given in the form of a specific, written 'Warranty' document. However, a warranty may also arise by operation of law based upon the seller's description of the goods, and perhaps their source and quality, and any material deviation from that specification would violate the guarantee.
   a. Office for Harmonization in the Internal Market
   b. Energy Star
   c. Imperial Group v. Philip Morris
   d. Express warranty

37. _____, in marketing, is the practice of modifying a basic list price based on the geographical location of the buyer. It is intended to reflect the costs of shipping to different locations.

## Chapter 9. Pricing: Understanding and Capturing Customer Value 75

There are several types of geographic pricing:

- FOB origin (Free on Board origin) - The shipping cost from the factory or warehouse is paid by the purchaser. Ownership of the goods is transferred to the buyer as soon as it leaves the point of origin. It can be either the buyer or seller that arranges for the transportation.
- Uniform delivery pricing - (also called postage stamp pricing) - The same price is charged to all.
- Zone pricing - Prices increase as shipping distances increase. This is sometimes done by drawing concentric circles on a map with the plant or warehouse at the center and each circle defining the boundary of a price zone. Instead of using circles, irregularly shaped price boundaries can be drawn that reflect geography, population density, transportation infrastructure, and shipping cost. (The term 'zone pricing' can also refer to the practice of setting prices that reflect local competitive conditions, i.e., the market forces of supply and demand, rather than actual cost of transportation.)

Zone pricing, as practiced in the gasoline industry in the United States, is the pricing of gasoline based on a complex and secret weighting of factors, such as the number of competing stations, number of vehicles, average traffic flow, population density, and geographic characteristics. This can result in two branded gas stations only a few miles apart selling gasoline at a price differential of as much as $0.50 per gallon.

a. Geographical pricing
b. Green market
c. Countervailing duties
d. Competitive

38. Why do retail stores need _____? With respect to the key objectives of growth and profit for any retail entity, _____ should significantly improve sales margins and increase sales by enabling the vendor to price variably and hence suitably and to control its product range based on profit margins. The retail stores will be able to compete more effectively with rivals in the form of mixed multiples, mail order and online retailers, who are often able to undercut but who do not generally have the same understanding of the retail market. In particular _____ is recognised as encouraging impulse buys, cross-selling of products and repeat sales.

a. 180SearchAssistant
b. Dynamic pricing
c. 6-3-5 Brainwriting
d. Power III

39. _____ or international commercial terms are a series of international sales terms widely used throughout the world. They are used to divide transaction costs and responsibilities between buyer and seller and reflect state-of-the-art transportation practices. They closely correspond to the U.N. Convention on Contracts for the International Sale of Goods.

a. ACNielsen
b. ADTECH
c. International trade
d. Incoterms

## Chapter 9. Pricing: Understanding and Capturing Customer Value

40. _____ - Prices increase as shipping distances increase. This is sometimes done by drawing concentric circles on a map with the plant or warehouse at the center and each circle defining the boundary of a price zone. Instead of using circles, irregularly shaped price boundaries can be drawn that reflect geography, population density, transportation infrastructure, and shipping cost. The term '_____' can also refer to the practice of setting prices that reflect local competitive conditions, i.e., the market forces of supply and demand, rather than actual cost of transportation.

_____, as practiced in the gasoline industry in the United States, is the pricing of gasoline based on a complex and secret weighting of factors, such as the number of competing stations, number of vehicles, average traffic flow, population density, and geographic characteristics. This can result in two branded gas stations only a few miles apart selling gasoline at a price differential of as much as $0.50 per gallon.

a. Geographical pricing
b. Safeguard
c. Countervailing duties
d. Zone pricing

41. The Oxford University Press defines _____ as 'marketing on a worldwide scale reconciling or taking commercial advantage of global operational differences, similarities and opportunities in order to meet global objectives.' Oxford University Press' Glossary of Marketing Terms.

Here are three reasons for the shift from domestic to _____ as given by the authors of the textbook, _____ Management--3rd Edition by Masaaki Kotabe and Kristiaan Helsen, 2004.

One of the product categories in which global competition has been easy to track is in U.S. automotive sales.

a. Relationship marketing
b. Cause-related Marketing
c. Guerrilla Marketing
d. Global marketing

42. _____ is the examining of goods or services from retailers with the intent to purchase at that time. _____ is an activity of selection and/or purchase. In some contexts it is considered a leisure activity as well as an economic one.
a. Hawkers
b. Khodebshchik
c. Discount store
d. Shopping

43. _____ is defined by the American _____ Association as the activity, set of institutions, and processes for creating, communicating, delivering, and exchanging offerings that have value for customers, clients, partners, and society at large. The term developed from the original meaning which referred literally to going to market, as in shopping, or going to a market to sell goods or services.

_____ practice tends to be seen as a creative industry, which includes advertising, distribution and selling.

a. Gatefold
b. Product naming
c. Marketing
d. Business marketing

44. The _____ of 1936 (or Anti-Price Discrimination Act, 15 U.S.C. § 13) is a United States federal law that prohibits what were considered, at the time of passage, to be anticompetitive practices by producers, specifically price discrimination. It grew out of practices in which chain stores were allowed to purchase goods at lower prices than other retailers.

a. Copyright infringement
b. Social Norms Approach
c. Trademark classification
d. Robinson-Patman Act

45. _____ is a sub-discipline and type of marketing. There are two main definitional characteristics which distinguish it from other types of marketing. The first is that it attempts to send its messages directly to consumers, without the use of intervening media.
a. Database marketing
b. Power III
c. Direct Marketing Associations
d. Direct marketing

46. _____ is the practice of selling a product or service at a very low price, intending to drive competitors out of the market, or create barriers to entry for potential new competitors. If competitors or potential competitors cannot sustain equal or lower prices without losing money, they go out of business or choose not to enter the business. The predatory merchant then has fewer competitors or is even a de facto monopoly, and can then raise prices above what the market would otherwise bear.
a. Power III
b. List price
c. Predatory pricing
d. 180SearchAssistant

47. _____ exists when sales of identical goods or services are transacted at different prices from the same provider. In a theoretical market with perfect information, no transaction costs or prohibition on secondary exchange (or re-selling) to prevent arbitrage, _____ can only be a feature of monopoly and oligopoly markets, where market power can be exercised. Otherwise, the moment the seller tries to sell the same good at different prices, the buyer at the lower price can arbitrage by selling to the consumer buying at the higher price but with a tiny discount.
a. Price maintenance
b. Relationship based pricing
c. Price discrimination
d. Price points

48. _____ is an agreement between business competitors to sell the same product or service at the same price. In general, it is an agreement intended to ultimately push the price of a product as high as possible, leading to profits for all the sellers. _____ can also involve any agreement to fix, peg, discount or stabilize prices.
a. Price competition
b. Non-price competition
c. Direct competition
d. Price fixing

49. Resale _____ is the practice whereby a manufacturer and its distributors agree that the latter will sell the former's product at certain prices (resale _____), at or above a price floor (minimum resale _____) or at or below a price ceiling (maximum resale _____.) These rules prevent resellers from competing too fiercely on price and thus drive down profits. Some argue that the manufacturer may do this because it wishes to keep resellers profitable, and thus keeping the manufacturer profitable.
a. Price war
b. Price maintenance
c. Premium pricing
d. Pricing

50. The _____ is an independent agency of the United States government, established in 1914 by the _____ Act. Its principal mission is the promotion of 'consumer protection' and the elimination and prevention of what regulators perceive to be harmfully 'anti-competitive' business practices, such as coercive monopoly.

The _____ Act was one of President Wilson's major acts against trusts.

a. Federal Trade Commission
b. 6-3-5 Brainwriting
c. Power III
d. 180SearchAssistant

## Chapter 10. Marketing Channels and Supply Chain Management

1. _____ is one of the four elements of marketing mix. An organization or set of organizations (go-betweens) involved in the process of making a product or service available for use or consumption by a consumer or business user.

The other three parts of the marketing mix are product, pricing, and promotion.

a. Clustering  
b. LIFO  
c. Better Living Through Chemistry  
d. Distribution

2. _____ is defined by the American _____ Association as the activity, set of institutions, and processes for creating, communicating, delivering, and exchanging offerings that have value for customers, clients, partners, and society at large. The term developed from the original meaning which referred literally to going to market, as in shopping, or going to a market to sell goods or services.

_____ practice tends to be seen as a creative industry, which includes advertising, distribution and selling.

a. Marketing  
b. Product naming  
c. Gatefold  
d. Business marketing

3. A _____ or logistics network is the system of organizations, people, technology, activities, information and resources involved in moving a product or service from supplier to customer. _____ activities transform natural resources, raw materials and components into a finished product that is delivered to the end customer. In sophisticated _____ systems, used products may re-enter the _____ at any point where residual value is recyclable.

a. Supply chain  
b. Supply chain network  
c. Megalister  
d. Wholesale

4. A personal and cultural _____ is a relative ethic _____, an assumption upon which implementation can be extrapolated. A _____ system is a set of consistent _____s and measures that is soo not true. A principle _____ is a foundation upon which other _____s and measures of integrity are based.

a. Dolly Dimples  
b. Value  
c. Customization  
d. Private branding

5. In economics, business, retail, and accounting, a _____ is the value of money that has been used up to produce something, and hence is not available for use anymore. In economics, a _____ is an alternative that is given up as a result of a decision. In business, the _____ may be one of acquisition, in which case the amount of money expended to acquire it is counted as _____.

a. Fixed costs  
b. Transaction cost  
c. Marginal cost  
d. Cost

6. _____ is a sub-discipline and type of marketing. There are two main definitional characteristics which distinguish it from other types of marketing. The first is that it attempts to send its messages directly to consumers, without the use of intervening media.

a. Database marketing  
b. Power III  
c. Direct marketing  
d. Direct Marketing Associations

7. _____ occurs when manufacturers (brands) disintermediate their channel partners, such as distributors, retailers, dealers, and sales representatives, by selling their products direct to consumers through general marketing methods and/or over the internet through eCommerce.

Some manufacturers want their brands to capture the power of the internet but do not want to create conflict with their other distribution channels, as these partners are necessary and viable for any manufacturer to maintain and gain success. The Census Bureau of the U.S. Department of Commerce reported that online sales in 2005 grew 24.6 percent over 2004 to reach 86.3 billion dollars.

a. Brand culture
b. Fitting Group
c. Brand loyalty
d. Channel conflict

8. The most important feature of a contract is that one party makes an _____ for an arrangement that another accepts. This can be called a 'concurrence of wills' or 'ad idem' (meeting of the minds) of two or more parties. The concept is somewhat contested.
a. ADTECH
b. Offer
c. ACNielsen
d. AMAX

9. Procter is a surname, and may also refer to:

- Bryan Waller Procter (pseud. Barry Cornwall), English poet
- Goodwin Procter, American law firm
- _____, consumer products multinational

a. Comparison-Shopping agent
b. Push
c. Developed country
d. Procter ' Gamble

10. In economics, _____ is the removal of intermediaries in a supply chain: 'cutting out the middleman'. Instead of going through traditional distribution channels, which had some type of intermediate (such as a distributor, wholesaler, broker, or agent), companies may now deal with every customer directly, for example via the Internet. One important factor is a drop in the cost of servicing customers directly.
a. Business-to-government
b. Recommender system
c. Disintermediation
d. Spam Lit

11. _____ is a broad label that refers to any individuals or households that use goods and services generated within the economy. The concept of a _____ is used in different contexts, so that the usage and significance of the term may vary.

A _____ is a person who uses any product or service.

a. Consumer
b. 180SearchAssistant
c. Power III
d. 6-3-5 Brainwriting

12. A _____ is a relatively new executive level position at a corporation, company, organization typically reporting directly to the CEO or board of directors. The _____ is responsible for a brand's image, experience, and promise, and propagating it throughout all aspects of the company. The brand officer oversees marketing, advertising, design, public relations and customer service departments.

a. Chief brand officer  
b. Chief executive officer  
c. Decision Analyst  
d. Power III

13. The Oxford University Press defines _____ as 'marketing on a worldwide scale reconciling or taking commercial advantage of global operational differences, similarities and opportunities in order to meet global objectives.' Oxford University Press' Glossary of Marketing Terms.

Here are three reasons for the shift from domestic to _____ as given by the authors of the textbook, _____ Management--3rd Edition by Masaaki Kotabe and Kristiaan Helsen, 2004.

One of the product categories in which global competition has been easy to track is in U.S. automotive sales.

a. Relationship marketing  
b. Global marketing  
c. Cause-related Marketing  
d. Guerrilla Marketing

14. _____ is a form of communication that typically attempts to persuade potential customers to purchase or to consume more of a particular brand of product or service. 'While now central to the contemporary global economy and the reproduction of global production networks, it is only quite recently that _____ has been more than a marginal influence on patterns of sales and production. The formation of modern _____ was intimately bound up with the emergence of new forms of monopoly capitalism around the end of the 19th and beginning of the 20th century as one element in corporate strategies to create, organize and where possible control markets, especially for mass produced consumer goods.

a. Advertising  
b. ADTECH  
c. AMAX  
d. ACNielsen

15. Customer _____ consists of the processes a company uses to track and organize its contacts with its current and prospective customers. CRelationship management software is used to support these processes; information about customers and customer interactions can be entered, stored and accessed by employees in different company departments. Typical CRelationship management goals are to improve services provided to customers, and to use customer contact information for targeted marketing.

a. Relationship management  
b. Corporate image  
c. Kano model  
d. Pinstorm

16. _____ consists of the processes a company uses to track and organize its contacts with its current and prospective customers. _____ software is used to support these processes; information about customers and customer interactions can be entered, stored and accessed by employees in different company departments. Typical _____ goals are to improve services provided to customers, and to use customer contact information for targeted marketing.

a. Customer relationship management  
b. Buy one, get one free  
c. Customer franchise  
d. Social marketing

17. _____ refers to when a retailer or wholesaler is 'tied' to purchase from a supplier on the understanding that no other distributor will be appointed or receive supplies in a given area. When the sales outlets are owned by the supplier, _____ is because of vertical integration, where the outlets are independent _____ is illegal due to the Restrictive Trade Practices Act, however, if it is registered and approved it is allowed.

_____ can be a barrier to entry, it can be defended on the grounds that it is beneficial to consumers as it can allow after sales service to be better.

a. ACNielsen
c. ADTECH
b. AMAX
d. Exclusive dealing

18. _____ is the management of the flow of goods, information and other resources, including energy and people, between the point of origin and the point of consumption in order to meet the requirements of consumers (frequently, and originally, military organizations.) _____ involves the integration of information, transportation, inventory, warehousing, material-handling, and packaging. _____ is a channel of the supply chain which adds the value of time and place utility.

a. Logistics
c. 6-3-5 Brainwriting
b. Power III
d. 180SearchAssistant

19. A _____ is a list of the general tasks and responsibilities of a position. Typically, it also includes to whom the position reports, specifications such as the qualifications needed by the person in the job, salary range for the position, etc. A _____ is usually developed by conducting a job analysis, which includes examining the tasks and sequences of tasks necessary to perform the job.

a. 6-3-5 Brainwriting
c. Power III
b. 180SearchAssistant
d. Job description

20. A _____ for a set of products is a warehouse or other specialized building, often with refrigeration or air conditioning, which is stocked with products (goods) to be re-distributed to retailers, wholesalers or directly to consumers. A _____ is a principle part, the 'order processing' element, of the entire 'order fulfillment' process. _____ s are usually thought of as being 'demand driven'.

a. 6-3-5 Brainwriting
c. Power III
b. 180SearchAssistant
d. Distribution center

21. _____ is a list for goods and materials held available in stock by a business. It is also used for a list of the contents of a household and for a list for testamentary purposes of the possessions of someone who has died. In accounting _____ is considered an asset.

a. ADTECH
c. ACNielsen
b. Ending Inventory
d. Inventory

22. _____ is an inventory strategy implemented to improve the return on investment of a business by reducing in-process inventory and its associated carrying costs. In order to achieve JIT the process must have signals of what is going on elsewhere within the process. This means that the process is often driven by a series of signals, which can be Kanban , that tell production processes when to make the next part.

a. Just-in-time
c. Sample sales
b. PlattForm, Inc.
d. Comprehensive,

23. _____ is the use of an object (typically referred to as an RFID tag) applied to or incorporated into a product, animal, or person for the purpose of identification and tracking using radio waves. Some tags can be read from several meters away and beyond the line of sight of the reader.

Most RFID tags contain at least two parts.

## Chapter 10. Marketing Channels and Supply Chain Management

a. 6-3-5 Brainwriting
b. Power III
c. 180SearchAssistant
d. Radio-frequency identification

24. _____ refers to the structured transmission of data between organizations by electronic means. It is used to transfer electronic documents from one computer system to another (ie) from one trading partner to another trading partner. It is more than mere E-mail; for instance, organizations might replace bills of lading and even checks with appropriate _____ messages.
   a. Electronic data interchange
   b. ADTECH
   c. AMAX
   d. ACNielsen

25. _____ is a family of business models in which the buyer of a product provides certain information to a supplier of that product and the supplier takes full responsibility for maintaining an agreed inventory of the material, usually at the buyer's consumption location (usually a store.) A third party logistics provider can also be involved to make sure that the buyer have the required level of inventory by adjusting the demand and supply gaps.

As a symbiotic relationship, _____ makes it less likely that a business will unintentionally become out of stock of a good and reduces inventory in the supply chain.

   a. Customer driven supply chain
   b. Vendor Managed Inventory
   c. Merchandise management system
   d. Fulfillment house

26. _____ refer to a collection of facts usually collected as the result of experience, observation or experiment or a set of premises. This may consist of numbers, words particularly as measurements or observations of a set of variables. _____ are often viewed as a lowest level of abstraction from which information and knowledge are derived.
   a. Data
   b. P-Value
   c. Randomization
   d. Median

27. _____ , according to The American Marketing Association, is 'a planning process designed to assure that all brand contacts received by a customer or prospect for a product, service, or organization are relevant to that person and consistent over time.' (Marketing Power Dictionary)

_____ is a term used to describe a holistic approach to marketing. It aims to ensure consistency of message and the complementary use of media. The concept includes online and offline marketing channels.

   a. ACNielsen
   b. ADTECH
   c. AMAX
   d. Integrated marketing communications

28. the term _____ is that part of Supply Chain Management that plans, implements, and controls the efficient, effective, forward, and reverse flow and storage of goods, services, and related information between the point of origin and the point of consumption in order to meet customers' requirements.

Software is used for logistics automation which helps the supply chain industry in automating the work flow as well as management of the system. There are very few generalized software available in the new market in the said topology.

## Chapter 10. Marketing Channels and Supply Chain Management

a. Performance measurement
c. Cash cow
b. Logistics management
d. Digital strategy

29. Radio-frequency identification (_____) is the use of an object (typically referred to as an _____ tag) applied to or incorporated into a product, animal, or person for the purpose of identification and tracking using radio waves. Some tags can be read from several meters away and beyond the line of sight of the reader.

Most _____ tags contain at least two parts.

a. Power III
c. 6-3-5 Brainwriting
b. 180SearchAssistant
d. RFID

30. _____ is a modern day comedy of cross-cultural conflict and romance, directed by John Jeffcoat, released in 2006.

Todd Anderson (Josh Hamilton) spends his days managing a customer call center for Western Novelty, an American novelty product company, in Seattle, until he and his entire department are _____ to India. Adding insult to injury, Todd is sent to India to train his replacement.

a. Outsourced
c. ADTECH
b. ACNielsen
d. AMAX

31. _____ is an advertisement in which a particular product specifically mentions a competitor by name for the express purpose of showing why the competitor is inferior to the product naming it.

This should not be confused with parody advertisements, where a fictional product is being advertised for the purpose of poking fun at the particular advertisement, nor should it be confused with the use of a coined brand name for the purpose of comparing the product without actually naming an actual competitor. ('Wikipedia tastes better and is less filling than the Encyclopedia Galactica.')

In the 1980s, during what has been referred to as the cola wars, soft-drink manufacturer Pepsi ran a series of advertisements where people, caught on hidden camera, in a blind taste test, chose Pepsi over rival Coca-Cola.

a. Comparative advertising
c. GL-70
b. Heavy-up
d. Cost per conversion

## Chapter 11. Retailing and Wholesaling

1. _____ consists of the sale of goods or merchandise from a fixed location, such as a department store or kiosk in small or individual lots for direct consumption by the purchaser. _____ may include subordinated services, such as delivery. Purchasers may be individuals or businesses.
   a. General line of merchandise
   b. Retailing
   c. Scrapstore
   d. Warehouse club

2. _____ is anything that is intended to save time, energy or frustration. A _____ store at a petrol station, for example, sells items that have nothing to do with gasoline/petrol, but it saves the consumer from having to go to a grocery store. '_____' is a very relative term and its meaning tends to change over time.
   a. Demographic profile
   b. Convenience
   c. Consumer confidence
   d. Multidimensional scaling

3. A _____ is a small store or shop that sells candy, ice-cream, soft drinks, lottery tickets, newspapers and magazines, along with a small selection of food and grocery supplies. Stores that are part of gas stations may also sell motor oil, windshield washer fluid, radiator fluid, and maps. Often toiletries and other hygiene products are stocked, and some of these stores also offer money orders and wire transfer services or liquor products.
   a. 180SearchAssistant
   b. Convenience store
   c. 6-3-5 Brainwriting
   d. Power III

4. A _____ is a retail establishment which specializes in selling a wide range of products without a single predominant merchandise line. _____s usually sell products including apparel, furniture, appliances, electronics, and additionally select other lines of products such as paint, hardware, toiletries, cosmetics, photographic equipment, jewelery, toys, and sporting goods. Certain _____s are further classified as discount _____s.
   a. 6-3-5 Brainwriting
   b. 180SearchAssistant
   c. Power III
   d. Department store

5. There are many important decisions about product and service development and marketing. In the process of product development and marketing we should focus on strategic decisions about product attributes, product branding, product packaging, product labeling and product support services. But product strategy also calls for building a _____.
   a. Product line
   b. Context analysis
   c. Prosumer
   d. Demand generation

6. _____ is an advertisement in which a particular product specifically mentions a competitor by name for the express purpose of showing why the competitor is inferior to the product naming it.

This should not be confused with parody advertisements, where a fictional product is being advertised for the purpose of poking fun at the particular advertisement, nor should it be confused with the use of a coined brand name for the purpose of comparing the product without actually naming an actual competitor. ('Wikipedia tastes better and is less filling than the Encyclopedia Galactica.')

In the 1980s, during what has been referred to as the cola wars, soft-drink manufacturer Pepsi ran a series of advertisements where people, caught on hidden camera, in a blind taste test, chose Pepsi over rival Coca-Cola.

   a. Cost per conversion
   b. Comparative advertising
   c. GL-70
   d. Heavy-up

7. _____ are small stores which specialize in a specific range of merchandise and related items. Most stores have an extensive width and depth of stock in the item that they specify in and provide high levels of service and expertise. The pricing policy is generally in the medium to high range, depending on factors like the type and exclusivity of merchandise and ownership, that is, whether they are owner operated or a chain operation which has the advantage of bulk purchasing and centralized warehousing system.
   a. Specialty stores
   b. History of pawnbroking
   c. Garage sale
   d. Go-backs

8. _____ is a term used in marketing and strategic management to describe a product, service, brand, or company that has such a distinct sustainable competitive advantage that competing firms find it almost impossible to operate profitably in that industry. The existence of a _____ will eliminate almost all market entities, whether real or virtual. Many existing firms will leave the industry, thereby increasing the industry's concentration ratio.
   a. 6-3-5 Brainwriting
   b. Category killer
   c. Power III
   d. 180SearchAssistant

9. In commerce, a _____ is a superstore which combines a supermarket and a department store. The result is a very large retail facility which carries an enormous range of products under one roof, including full lines of groceries and general merchandise. In theory, _____s allow customers to satisfy all their routine weekly shopping needs in one trip.
   a. 180SearchAssistant
   b. Power III
   c. Hypermarket
   d. 6-3-5 Brainwriting

10. _____ in economics and business is the result of an exchange and from that trade we assign a numerical monetary value to a good, service or asset. If I trade 4 apples for an orange, the _____ of an orange is 4 - apples. Inversely, the _____ of an apple is 1/4 oranges.
    a. Contribution margin-based pricing
    b. Price
    c. Price war
    d. Transfer pricing

11. A _____ is a type of department store, which sell products at prices lower than those asked by traditional retail outlets. Most discount department stores offer wide assortments of goods; others specialize in such merchandise as jewelry, electronic equipment, or electrical appliances. _____s are not dollar stores, which sell goods at a dollar or less.
    a. Garage sale
    b. Brick and mortar business
    c. Junk shop
    d. Discount store

12. A personal and cultural _____ is a relative ethic _____, an assumption upon which implementation can be extrapolated. A _____ system is a set of consistent _____s and measures that is soo not true. A principle _____ is a foundation upon which other _____s and measures of integrity are based.
    a. Private branding
    b. Value
    c. Dolly Dimples
    d. Customization

13. A _____ is a commercial building for storage of goods. _____s are used by manufacturers, importers, exporters, wholesalers, transport businesses, customs, etc. They are usually large plain buildings in industrial areas of cities and towns.
    a. 180SearchAssistant
    b. Power III
    c. 6-3-5 Brainwriting
    d. Warehouse

## Chapter 11. Retailing and Wholesaling

14. A _____ is a retail store, usually selling a wide variety of merchandise, in which customers pay annual membership fees in order to shop. The clubs are able to keep prices low due to the no-frills format of the stores. In addition, customers are required to buy large, wholesale quantities of the store's products, which makes these clubs attractive to both bargain hunters and small business owners.

- a. Same-store sales
- b. General line of merchandise
- c. Sales per unit area
- d. Warehouse club

15. Wholesaling, historically called jobbing, is the sale of goods or merchandise to retailers, to industrial, commercial, institutional or to other wholesalers and related subordinated services.

According to the United Nations Statistics Division, '_____' is the resale (sale without transformation) of new and used goods to retailers, to industrial, commercial, institutional or professional users or involves acting as an agent or broker in buying merchandise for such persons or companies. Wholesalers frequently physically assemble, sort and grade goods in large lots, break bulk, repack and redistribute in smaller lots.

- a. Wholesale
- b. Supply network
- c. Purchasing
- d. Megalister

16. _____ are retail outlets, usually corporate owned businesses, that share brands and central management, often with standardized business methods and practices, and these may include stores, restaurants, and some service-oriented businesses.

The displacement of independent businesses by chains has generated controversy in many countries, and has sparked increased collaboration among independent businesses and communities to prevent chain proliferation. Such efforts occur within national trade groups such as the American Booksellers Association, as well as community-based coalitions such as Independent Business Alliances.

- a. Price-weighted
- b. Supplier diversity
- c. Product life cycle management
- d. Chain stores

17. A _____ is defined by the International Co-operative Alliance's Statement on the Co-operative Identity as an autonomous association of persons united voluntarily to meet their common economic, social, and cultural needs and aspirations through a jointly-owned and democratically-controlled enterprise. It is a business organization owned and operated by a group of individuals for their mutual benefit. A _____ may also be defined as a business owned and controlled equally by the people who use its services or who work at it.

- a. 180SearchAssistant
- b. 6-3-5 Brainwriting
- c. Power III
- d. Cooperative

18. A _____ is a collection of symbols, experiences and associations connected with a product, a service, a person or any other artifact or entity.

_____s have become increasingly important components of culture and the economy, now being described as 'cultural accessories and personal philosophies'.

Some people distinguish the psychological aspect of a _____ from the experiential aspect.

a. Naming rights  
b. Lovemarks  
c. Status brand  
d. Brand

19. _____ refers to the methods, practices and operations conducted to promote and sustain certain categories of commercial activity. The term is understood to have different specific meanings depending on the context. Merchandise is a sale goods at a store

In marketing, one of the definitions of _____ is the practice in which the brand or image from one product or service is used to sell another.

a. Merchandise  
b. Word of mouth  
c. Marketing communication  
d. Merchandising

20. _____ is defined by the American _____ Association as the activity, set of institutions, and processes for creating, communicating, delivering, and exchanging offerings that have value for customers, clients, partners, and society at large. The term developed from the original meaning which referred literally to going to market, as in shopping, or going to a market to sell goods or services.

_____ practice tends to be seen as a creative industry, which includes advertising, distribution and selling.

a. Gatefold  
b. Marketing  
c. Business marketing  
d. Product naming

21. _____ was originally coined by Austrian psychologist Alfred Adler in 1929. The current broader sense of the word dates from 1961.

In sociology, a _____ is the way a person lives.

a. 6-3-5 Brainwriting  
b. 180SearchAssistant  
c. Power III  
d. Lifestyle

22. _____ is a super-regional shopping mall located in the Twin Cities suburb of Bloomington, Minnesota. The mall is located southeast of the junction of Interstate 494 and Minnesota State Highway 77, north of the Minnesota River and is across the interstate from the Minneapolis-St. Paul International Airport. In the United States, it is the second largest enclosed mall in terms of retail space but is largest in terms of total enclosed floor area.

a. 180SearchAssistant  
b. Mall of America  
c. 6-3-5 Brainwriting  
d. Power III

23. _____ is one of the four Ps of the marketing mix. The other three aspects are product, promotion, and place. It is also a key variable in microeconomic price allocation theory.

a. Pricing  
b. Cost-plus pricing  
c. Resale price maintenance  
d. Transfer pricing

24. A _____ is an open area shopping center where the stores are arranged in a row, with a sidewalk in front. _____s are typically developed as a unit and have large parking lots in front. They face major traffic arterials and tend to be self-contained with few pedestrian connections to surrounding neighborhoods.

## Chapter 11. Retailing and Wholesaling

a. Charity shop
b. Gruen transfer
c. Sales per unit area
d. Strip mall

25. _____ is the examining of goods or services from retailers with the intent to purchase at that time. _____ is an activity of selection and/or purchase. In some contexts it is considered a leisure activity as well as an economic one.
   a. Discount store
   b. Hawkers
   c. Shopping
   d. Khodebshchik

26. A _____ is a shopping center or mixed-used commercial development that combines the traditional retail functions of a shopping mall but with leisure amenities oriented towards upscale consumers. _____s, which were first labeled as such by Memphis developers Poag and McEwen in the late 1980s and emerged as a retailing trend in the late 1990s, are sometimes labeled 'boutique malls'. They are often located in affluent suburban areas.
   a. Lifestyle center
   b. Japan Advertising Photographers' Association
   c. Lobbying and Disclosure Act of 1995
   d. Retail floor planning

27. Procter is a surname, and may also refer to:

   - Bryan Waller Procter (pseud. Barry Cornwall), English poet
   - Goodwin Procter, American law firm
   - _____, consumer products multinational

   a. Comparison-Shopping agent
   b. Push
   c. Procter ' Gamble
   d. Developed country

28. A _____ is a party that mediates between a buyer and a seller. A _____ who also acts as a seller or as a buyer becomes a principal party to the deal. Distinguish agent: one who acts on behalf of a principal.
   a. 180SearchAssistant
   b. Professional services
   c. Power III
   d. Broker

29. _____s function as professionals who deal with trade, dealing in commodities that they do not produce themselves, in order to produce profit.

   _____s can be of two types:

   1. A wholesale _____ operates in the chain between producer and retail _____. Some wholesale _____s only organize the movement of goods rather than move the goods themselves.
   2. A retail _____ or retailer, sells commodities to consumers (including businesses.) A shop owner is a retail _____.

   A _____ class characterizes many pre-modern societies. Its status can range from high (even achieving titles like that of _____ prince or nabob) to low, such as in Chinese culture, due to the soiling capabilities of profiting from 'mere' trade, rather than from the labor of others reflected in agricultural produce, craftsmanship, and tribute.

## Chapter 11. Retailing and Wholesaling

In the United States, '_____' is defined (under the Uniform Commercial Code) as any person while engaged in a business or profession or a seller who deals regularly in the type of goods sold.

a. Merchant
c. Retail loss prevention

b. Countertrade
d. Trade credit

30. The _____ is generally accepted as the use and specification of the four p's describing the strategic position of a product in the marketplace. One version of the origins of the _____ starts in 1948 when James Culliton said that a marketing decision should be a result of something similar to a recipe. This version continued in 1953 when Neil Borden, in his American Marketing Association presidential address, took the recipe idea one step further and coined the term 'Marketing-Mix'.

a. Power III
c. 6-3-5 Brainwriting

b. 180SearchAssistant
d. Marketing mix

31. The _____ is a trilateral trade bloc in North America created by the governments of the United States, Canada, and Mexico. It superseded the Canada-United States Free Trade Agreement between the US and Canada.

Following diplomatic negotiations dating back to 1990 between the three nations, the leaders met in San Antonio, Texas on December 17, 1992 to sign _____.

a. 6-3-5 Brainwriting
c. Power III

b. North American Free Trade Agreement
d. 180SearchAssistant

32. _____ is a chain of 65 supermarkets in Baltimore, Northern Virginia and Washington, D.C. areas. Shoppers has fresh produce, Swift Angus beef, Smithfield natural pork, all-natural chicken, Dietz ' Watson delis, fresh seafood, steamed shrimp, as well as hot foods, full service pharmacies and in store full service banks.

Shoppers is thought to have derived several now-common supermarket features, such as warehouse shelving, open-bin bulk foods, large salad bars with hot prepared foods and specialized fans to keep produce fresh, and 'warehouse-sized' packaged products.

a. Product manager
c. Chief privacy officer

b. Shoppers Food ' Pharmacy
d. Raw data

## Chapter 12. Communicating Customer Value: Advertising, Sales Promotion, and Public Relations

1. _____ is a form of communication that typically attempts to persuade potential customers to purchase or to consume more of a particular brand of product or service. 'While now central to the contemporary global economy and the reproduction of global production networks, it is only quite recently that _____ has been more than a marginal influence on patterns of sales and production. The formation of modern _____ was intimately bound up with the emergence of new forms of monopoly capitalism around the end of the 19th and beginning of the 20th century as one element in corporate strategies to create, organize and where possible control markets, especially for mass produced consumer goods.

   a. ADTECH  
   b. AMAX  
   c. ACNielsen  
   d. Advertising  

2. _____ is a magazine, delivering news, analysis and data on marketing and media. The magazine was started as a broadsheet newspaper in Chicago in 1930. Today, its content appears in a print weekly distributed around the world and on many electronic platforms, including: AdAge.com, daily e-mail newsletters called Ad Age Daily, Ad Age's Mediaworks and Ad Age Digital; weekly newsletters such as Madison ' Vine (about branded entertainment) and Ad Age China; podcasts called Why It Matters and various videos.

   a. Ethical Consumer  
   b. Adweek  
   c. Entrepreneur magazine  
   d. Advertising Age  

3. _____ is a sub-discipline and type of marketing. There are two main definitional characteristics which distinguish it from other types of marketing. The first is that it attempts to send its messages directly to consumers, without the use of intervening media.

   a. Database marketing  
   b. Direct Marketing Associations  
   c. Power III  
   d. Direct marketing  

4. _____ is defined by the American _____ Association as the activity, set of institutions, and processes for creating, communicating, delivering, and exchanging offerings that have value for customers, clients, partners, and society at large. The term developed from the original meaning which referred literally to going to market, as in shopping, or going to a market to sell goods or services.

   _____ practice tends to be seen as a creative industry, which includes advertising, distribution and selling.

   a. Gatefold  
   b. Product naming  
   c. Business marketing  
   d. Marketing  

5. _____ refers to messages and related media used to communicate with a market. Those who practice advertising, branding, direct marketing, graphic design, marketing, packaging, promotion, publicity, sponsorship, public relations, sales, sales promotion and online marketing are termed marketing communicators, _____ managers, or more briefly as marcom managers.

   a. Word of mouth  
   b. Marketing communication  
   c. Merchandising  
   d. New Media Strategies

## Chapter 12. Communicating Customer Value: Advertising, Sales Promotion, and Public Relations

6. _____ involves disseminating information about a product, product line, brand, or company. It is one of the four key aspects of the marketing mix. (The other three elements are product marketing, pricing, and distribution). P>_____ is generally sub-divided into two parts:

- Above the line _____: Promotion in the media (e.g. TV, radio, newspapers, Internet and Mobile Phones) in which the advertiser pays an advertising agency to place the ad
- Below the line _____: All other _____. Much of this is intended to be subtle enough for the consumer to be unaware that _____ is taking place. E.g. sponsorship, product placement, endorsements, sales _____, merchandising, direct mail, personal selling, public relations, trade shows

a. Cash and carry
b. Technology maturity lifecycle
c. M80
d. Promotion

7. _____ is the practice of managing the flow of information between an organization and its publics. _____ - often referred to as _____ - gains an organization or individual exposure to their audiences using topics of public interest and news items that do not require direct payment. Because _____ places exposure in credible third-party outlets, it offers a third-party legitimacy that advertising does not have.

a. Power III
b. Symbolic analysis
c. Public relations
d. Graphic communication

8. _____ is one of the four aspects of promotional mix. (The other three parts of the promotional mix are advertising, personal selling, and publicity/public relations.) Media and non-media marketing communication are employed for a pre-determined, limited time to increase consumer demand, stimulate market demand or improve product availability.

a. Word of mouth
b. Merchandising
c. Sales promotion
d. New Media Strategies

9. _____ generally refers to a list of all planned expenses and revenues. It is a plan for saving and spending. A _____ is an important concept in microeconomics, which uses a _____ line to illustrate the trade-offs between two or more goods.

a. Power III
b. 6-3-5 Brainwriting
c. Budget
d. 180SearchAssistant

10. _____, according to The American Marketing Association, is 'a planning process designed to assure that all brand contacts received by a customer or prospect for a product, service, or organization are relevant to that person and consistent over time.' (Marketing Power Dictionary)

_____ is a term used to describe a holistic approach to marketing. It aims to ensure consistency of message and the complementary use of media. The concept includes online and offline marketing channels.

a. Integrated marketing communications
b. AMAX
c. ACNielsen
d. ADTECH

11. A personal and cultural _____ is a relative ethic _____, an assumption upon which implementation can be extrapolated. A _____ system is a set of consistent _____s and measures that is soo not true. A principle _____ is a foundation upon which other _____s and measures of integrity are based.

## Chapter 12. Communicating Customer Value: Advertising, Sales Promotion, and Public Relations

a. Private branding
c. Dolly Dimples
b. Customization
d. Value

12. _____ is a market coverage strategy in which a firm decides to ignore market segment differences and go after the whole market with one offer.it is type of marketing (or attempting to sell through persuasion) of a product to a wide audience. The idea is to broadcast a message that will reach the largest number of people possible. Traditionally _____ has focused on radio, television and newspapers as the medium used to reach this broad audience.

a. Mass marketing
c. Product naming
b. Value chain
d. Business-to-consumer

13. _____ has traditionally been understood as the dissemination of information (usually by radio or television) to a narrow audience, not to the general public. Some forms of _____ involve directional signals or use of encryption. In the context of out-of-home advertising, this term often refers to the display of content on a digital signage network.

a. Narrowcasting
c. Promotional mix
b. Chief privacy officer
d. Wells Fargo ' Co.

14. Procter is a surname, and may also refer to:

- Bryan Waller Procter (pseud. Barry Cornwall), English poet
- Goodwin Procter, American law firm
- _____, consumer products multinational

a. Comparison-Shopping agent
c. Push
b. Developed country
d. Procter ' Gamble

15. A _____ is a collection of symbols, experiences and associations connected with a product, a service, a person or any other artifact or entity.

_____s have become increasingly important components of culture and the economy, now being described as 'cultural accessories and personal philosophies'.

Some people distinguish the psychological aspect of a _____ from the experiential aspect.

a. Lovemarks
c. Status brand
b. Naming rights
d. Brand

16. _____ is a term commonly used to describe commerce transactions between businesses like the one between a manufacturer and a wholesaler or a wholesaler and a retailer i.e both the buyer and the seller are business entity.This is unlike business-to-consumers (B2C) which involve a business entity and end consumer, or business-to-government (B2G) which involve a business entity and government.

The volume of B2B transactions is much higher than the volume of B2C transactions. The primary reason for this is that in a typical supply chain there will be many B2B transactions involving subcomponent or raw materials, and only one B2C transaction, specifically sale of the finished product to the end customer.

## Chapter 12. Communicating Customer Value: Advertising, Sales Promotion, and Public Relations

a. Customer analytics
c. Disruptive technology
b. Cannibalization
d. Business-to-business

17. The business terms _____ and pull originated in the logistic and supply chain management, but are also widely used in marketing.

A _____-pull-system in business describes the move of a product or information between two subjects. On markets the consumers usually 'pulls' the goods or information they demand for their needs, while the offerers or suppliers '_____es' them toward the consumers.

a. Rural market
c. Rebate
b. Procter ' Gamble
d. Push

18. A _____ is a plan of action designed to achieve a particular goal.

_____ is different from tactics. In military terms, tactics is concerned with the conduct of an engagement while _____ is concerned with how different engagements are linked.

a. 180SearchAssistant
c. Power III
b. Strategy
d. 6-3-5 Brainwriting

19. In grammar, the _____ is the form of an adjective or adverb which denotes the degree or grade by which a person, thing and is used in this context with a subordinating conjunction, such as than, as...as, etc.

The structure of a _____ in English consists normally of the positive form of the adjective or adverb, plus the suffix -er e.g. 'he is taller than his father is', or 'the village is less picturesque than the town nearby'.

a. Comparative
c. 6-3-5 Brainwriting
b. 180SearchAssistant
d. Power III

20. _____ is an advertisement in which a particular product specifically mentions a competitor by name for the express purpose of showing why the competitor is inferior to the product naming it.

This should not be confused with parody advertisements, where a fictional product is being advertised for the purpose of poking fun at the particular advertisement, nor should it be confused with the use of a coined brand name for the purpose of comparing the product without actually naming an actual competitor. ('Wikipedia tastes better and is less filling than the Encyclopedia Galactica.')

In the 1980s, during what has been referred to as the cola wars, soft-drink manufacturer Pepsi ran a series of advertisements where people, caught on hidden camera, in a blind taste test, chose Pepsi over rival Coca-Cola.

a. GL-70
c. Cost per conversion
b. Heavy-up
d. Comparative advertising

## Chapter 12. Communicating Customer Value: Advertising, Sales Promotion, and Public Relations

21. _____ is when advertising is carried out in an informative manner Also, _____ tends to help generate a good reputation.

In some circumstances a business might be required to run _____ as part of resolving a law suit. Tobacco companies are one of the more notable examples of this.

a. Out-of-home advertising  
c. Informative advertising  
b. ACNielsen  
d. ADTECH

22. _____ is a form of social influence. It is the process of guiding people toward the adoption of an idea, attitude, or action by rational and symbolic (though not always logical) means. It is strategy of problem-solving relying on 'appeals' rather than coercion.

a. 6-3-5 Brainwriting  
c. 180SearchAssistant  
b. Power III  
d. Persuasion

23. _____ is the pioneer of the digital video recorder . _____ was introduced in the United States, and is now available in Canada, Mexico, Australia, and Taiwan. Created by _____, Inc..

a. Power III  
c. 180SearchAssistant  
b. 6-3-5 Brainwriting  
d. TiVo

24. _____ is the combination of an audio-visual program and a brand. It can be initiated either by the brand or by the broadcaster.

a. Status brand  
c. Branded entertainment  
b. Web 2.0  
d. Distinctiveness

25. _____ is a form of advertisement, where branded goods or services are placed in a context usually devoid of ads, such as movies, the story line of television shows Broadcasting ' Cable reported, 'Two thirds of advertisers employ 'branded entertainment'--_____--with the vast majority of that (80%) in commercial TV programming.' The story, based on a survey by the Association of National Advertisers, added, 'Reasons for using in-show plugs varied from 'stronger emotional connection' to better dovetailing with relevant content, to targetting a specific group.'

_____ became common in the 1980s, but can be traced back to the nineteenth century in publishing.

a. Power III  
c. 6-3-5 Brainwriting  
b. Product placement  
d. 180SearchAssistant

26. _____ was originally coined by Austrian psychologist Alfred Adler in 1929. The current broader sense of the word dates from 1961.

In sociology, a _____ is the way a person lives.

a. 180SearchAssistant  
c. 6-3-5 Brainwriting  
b. Power III  
d. Lifestyle

## Chapter 12. Communicating Customer Value: Advertising, Sales Promotion, and Public Relations

27. In promotion and of advertising, a _____ or endorsement consists of a written or spoken statement, sometimes from a person figure, sometimes from a private citizen, extolling the virtue of some product. The term '_____' most commonly applies to the sales-pitches attributed to ordinary citizens, whereas 'endorsement' usually applies to pitches by celebrities. See also Testify, Testimony, for historical context and etymology.
   a. Promotional items
   b. Testimonial
   c. Roll-in
   d. Promotional products

28. _____ is a job title in an advertising agency or media planning and buying agency, responsible for selecting media for advertisement placement on behalf of their clients. The main aim of a _____ is to assist their client in achieving business objectives through their advertising budgets by recommending the best possible use of various media platforms available to advertisers. Their roles may include analyzing target audiences, keeping abreast of media developments, reading market trends and understanding motivations of consumers (often including psychology and neuroscience.)
   a. Johnson Box
   b. Helicopter banner
   c. Mobile phone content advertising
   d. Media planner

29. _____ are media (newspapers, radio, television, movies, Internet, etc.) which are alternatives to the business or government-owned mass media. Proponents of _____ argue that the mainstream media are biased.
   a. ACNielsen
   b. Alternative media
   c. AMAX
   d. ADTECH

30. _____ is an employment website owned by Monster Worldwide. Monster is one of the 20 most visited websites out of 100 million worldwide, according to comScore Media Metrics (November 2006.) It was created in 1999 by the merger of The Monster Board (TMB) and Online Career Center (OCC), which were two of the first and most popular career web sites on the Internet.
   a. Power III
   b. 180SearchAssistant
   c. 6-3-5 Brainwriting
   d. Monster.com

31. The _____ is an English-language international daily newspaper published by Dow Jones ' Company in New York City with Asian and European editions. As of 2007, It has a worldwide daily circulation of more than 2 million, with approximately 931,000 paying online subscribers. It was the largest-circulation newspaper in the United States until November 2003, when it was surpassed by USA Today.
   a. Power III
   b. 180SearchAssistant
   c. 6-3-5 Brainwriting
   d. Wall Street Journal

32. An _____ or ad agency is a service business dedicated to creating, planning and handling advertising (and sometimes other forms of promotion) for its clients. An ad agency is independent from the client and provides an outside point of view to the effort of selling the client's products or services. An agency can also handle overall marketing and branding strategies and sales promotions for its clients.
   a. Advertising research
   b. Openad
   c. Advertising agency
   d. Onsert

33. The Oxford University Press defines _____ as 'marketing on a worldwide scale reconciling or taking commercial advantage of global operational differences, similarities and opportunities in order to meet global objectives.' Oxford University Press' Glossary of Marketing Terms.

## Chapter 12. Communicating Customer Value: Advertising, Sales Promotion, and Public Relations

Here are three reasons for the shift from domestic to _____ as given by the authors of the textbook, _____ Management--3rd Edition by Masaaki Kotabe and Kristiaan Helsen, 2004.

One of the product categories in which global competition has been easy to track is in U.S. automotive sales.

a. Relationship marketing  
c. Guerrilla Marketing  
b. Cause-related Marketing  
d. Global marketing

34. A _____ is a relatively new executive level position at a corporation, company, organization typically reporting directly to the CEO or board of directors. The _____ is responsible for a brand's image, experience, and promise, and propagating it throughout all aspects of the company. The brand officer oversees marketing, advertising, design, public relations and customer service departments.
   a. Power III
   b. Decision Analyst
   c. Chief brand officer
   d. Chief executive officer

35. _____ is a broad label that refers to any individuals or households that use goods and services generated within the economy. The concept of a _____ is used in different contexts, so that the usage and significance of the term may vary.

A _____ is a person who uses any product or service.

   a. 6-3-5 Brainwriting
   b. 180SearchAssistant
   c. Power III
   d. Consumer

36. In marketing a _____ is a ticket or document that can be exchanged for a financial discount or rebate when purchasing a product. Customarily, _____s are issued by manufacturers of consumer packaged goods or by retailers, to be used in retail stores as a part of sales promotions. They are often widely distributed through mail, magazines, newspapers, the Internet, and mobile devices such as cell phones.
   a. New Media Strategies
   b. Merchandising
   c. Marketing communication
   d. Coupon

37. _____ in economics and business is the result of an exchange and from that trade we assign a numerical monetary value to a good, service or asset. If I trade 4 apples for an orange, the _____ of an orange is 4 - apples. Inversely, the _____ of an apple is 1/4 oranges.
   a. Contribution margin-based pricing
   b. Price
   c. Transfer pricing
   d. Price war

38. _____ refers to articles of merchandise that are used in marketing and communication programs. These items are usually imprinted with a company's name, logo or slogan, and given away at trade shows, conferences, and as part of guerrilla marketing campaigns.

Almost anything can be branded with a company's name or logo and used for promotion.

## Chapter 12. Communicating Customer Value: Advertising, Sales Promotion, and Public Relations

a. Roll-in
b. Promotional products
c. Transpromotional
d. Promotional items

39. A _____ is an amount paid by way of reduction, return, or refund on what has already been paid or contributed. It is a type of sales promotion marketers use primarily as incentives or supplements to product sales. The mail-in _____ is the most common.
a. Convergent
b. Package-on-Package
c. Market specialization
d. Rebate

40. In the United States consumer sales promotions known as _____ or simply sweeps (both single and plural) have become associated with marketing promotions targeted toward both generating enthusiasm and providing incentive reactions among customers by enticing consumers to submit free entries into drawings of chance (and not skill) that are tied to product or service awareness wherein the featured prizes are given away by sponsoring companies. Prizes can vary in value from less than one dollar to more than one million U.S. dollars and can be in the form of cash, cars, homes, electronics, etc.

_____ frequently have eligibility limited by international, national, state, local, or other geographical factors.

a. Bitcom
b. Product line
c. Sweepstakes
d. Distributed presence

41. The _____ is a term used in economics to describe a good that is not scarce. A _____ is available in as great a quantity as desired with zero opportunity cost to society.

A good that is made available at zero price is not necessarily a _____.

a. Power III
b. Luxury good
c. Durable good
d. Free good

42. In economics and sociology, an _____ is any factor (financial or non-financial) that enables or motivates a particular course of action, or counts as a reason for preferring one choice to the alternatives. It is an expectation that encourages people to behave in a certain way. Since human beings are purposeful creatures, the study of _____ structures is central to the study of all economic activity (both in terms of individual decision-making and in terms of co-operation and competition within a larger institutional structure.)
a. AMAX
b. ACNielsen
c. ADTECH
d. Incentive

43. A trade fair (trade show or expo) is an exhibition organized so that companies in a specific industry can showcase and demonstrate their latest products, service, study activities of rivals and examine recent trends and opportunities. Some trade fairs are open to the public, while others can only be attended by company representatives (members of the trade) and members of the press, therefore _____ are classified as either 'Public' or 'Trade Only'. They are held on a continuing basis in virtually all markets and normally attract companies from around the globe.
a. 180SearchAssistant
b. Trade shows
c. 6-3-5 Brainwriting
d. Power III

## Chapter 12. Communicating Customer Value: Advertising, Sales Promotion, and Public Relations

44. _____ is anything that is generally accepted as payment for goods and services and repayment of debts. The main uses of _____ are as a medium of exchange, a unit of account, and a store of value. Some authors explicitly require _____ to be a standard of deferred payment.

   a. Perfect competition  
   b. Money  
   c. Law of demand  
   d. Market structure

45. _____ or simply buzz is a term used in word-of-mouth marketing. The interaction of consumers and users of a product or service serve to amplify the original marketing message.

   Some describe buzz as a form of hype among consumers, a vague but positive association, excitement, or anticipation about a product or service.

   a. Compliance professional  
   b. Marketing buzz  
   c. Shopping Neutral  
   d. Consumption smoothing

46. In marketing, a _____ is the 'persona' of a corporation which is designed to accord with and facilitate the attainment of business objectives. It is usually visibly manifested by way of branding and the use of trademarks.

   _____ comes into being when there is a common ownership of an organisational philosophy that is manifest in a distinct corporate culture -- the corporate personality.

   a. Naming rights  
   b. Corporate identity  
   c. Retail design  
   d. Brand implementation

## Chapter 13. Communicating Customer Value: Personal Selling and Direct Marketing

1. _____ is an advertisement in which a particular product specifically mentions a competitor by name for the express purpose of showing why the competitor is inferior to the product naming it.

This should not be confused with parody advertisements, where a fictional product is being advertised for the purpose of poking fun at the particular advertisement, nor should it be confused with the use of a coined brand name for the purpose of comparing the product without actually naming an actual competitor. ('Wikipedia tastes better and is less filling than the Encyclopedia Galactica.')

In the 1980s, during what has been referred to as the cola wars, soft-drink manufacturer Pepsi ran a series of advertisements where people, caught on hidden camera, in a blind taste test, chose Pepsi over rival Coca-Cola.

a. Cost per conversion
b. Heavy-up
c. GL-70
d. Comparative advertising

2. Procter is a surname, and may also refer to:

- Bryan Waller Procter (pseud. Barry Cornwall), English poet
- Goodwin Procter, American law firm
- _____, consumer products multinational

a. Comparison-Shopping agent
b. Push
c. Procter ' Gamble
d. Developed country

3. A _____ is a plan of action designed to achieve a particular goal.

_____ is different from tactics. In military terms, tactics is concerned with the conduct of an engagement while _____ is concerned with how different engagements are linked.

a. 180SearchAssistant
b. Power III
c. Strategy
d. 6-3-5 Brainwriting

4. _____s can refer to a method of trading sometimes used by organizations when procuring large contracts for goods and/or services where the customer takes control of the selling process by issuing a Request for Proposal and requiring a proposal response from previously identified or interested suppliers. _____s involve long sales cycles with multiple decision makers. Multiple stakeholders and stakeholder groups contribute to every _____.

a. Complex sale
b. Procter ' Gamble
c. Hospitality point of sales systems
d. Gold Key Matching Service

5. _____ is a global document management company which manufactures and sells a range of color and black-and-white printers, multifunction systems, photo copiers, digital production printing presses, and related consulting services and supplies. Xerox is headquartered in Norwalk, Connecticut , though its largest population of employees is based in and around Rochester, New York, the area in which the company was founded. The Xerox 914 was the first one-piece plain paper photocopier, and sold in the thousands.

Xerox was founded in 1906 in Rochester, New York as 'The Haloid Company', which originally manufactured photographic paper and equipment.

## Chapter 13. Communicating Customer Value: Personal Selling and Direct Marketing

a. Xerox Corporation
b. Japan Advertising Photographers' Association
c. Green Earth Market
d. Partnership for a Drug-Free America

6. _____ is exchange of capital, goods, and services across international borders or territories. In most countries, it represents a significant share of gross domestic product (GDP.) While _____ has been present throughout much of history, its economic, social, and political importance has been on the rise in recent centuries.
   a. ADTECH
   b. Incoterms
   c. ACNielsen
   d. International trade

7. _____ is the set of reasons that determines one to engage in a particular behavior. The term is generally used for human _____ but, theoretically, it can be used to describe the causes for animal behavior as well
   a. Power III
   b. 180SearchAssistant
   c. Role playing
   d. Motivation

8. Sales force management systems are information systems used in marketing and management that help automate some sales and sales force management functions. They are frequently combined with a marketing information system, in which case they are often called Customer Relationship Management (CRM) systems.

   _____ Systems, typically a part of a company's customer relationship management system, is a system that automatically records all the stages in a sales process.

   a. 6-3-5 Brainwriting
   b. 180SearchAssistant
   c. Power III
   d. Sales force automation

9. Sales force management systems are information systems used in marketing and management that help automate some sales and sales force management functions. They are frequently combined with a marketing information system, in which case they are often called Customer Relationship Management (CRM) systems.

   _____, typically a part of a company's customer relationship management system, is a system that automatically records all the stages in a sales process.

   a. Sales force automation systems
   b. Power III
   c. 6-3-5 Brainwriting
   d. 180SearchAssistant

10. In economics and sociology, an _____ is any factor (financial or non-financial) that enables or motivates a particular course of action, or counts as a reason for preferring one choice to the alternatives. It is an expectation that encourages people to behave in a certain way. Since human beings are purposeful creatures, the study of _____ structures is central to the study of all economic activity (both in terms of individual decision-making and in terms of co-operation and competition within a larger institutional structure.)
    a. ADTECH
    b. AMAX
    c. ACNielsen
    d. Incentive

11. In accounting, _____ has a very specific meaning. It is an outflow of cash or other valuable assets from a person or company to another person or company. This outflow of cash is generally one side of a trade for products or services that have equal or better current or future value to the buyer than to the seller.

## Chapter 13. Communicating Customer Value: Personal Selling and Direct Marketing

a. ADTECH
b. AMAX
c. ACNielsen
d. Expense

12. _____ is the physical search for minerals, fossils, precious metals or mineral specimens, and is also known as fossicking.

_____ is synonymous in some ways with mineral exploration which is an organised, large scale and at least semi-scientific effort undertaken by mineral resource companies to find commercially viable ore deposits. To actually be considered a prospector you must become registered as a professional prospector.

a. 6-3-5 Brainwriting
b. Power III
c. Prospecting
d. 180SearchAssistant

13. _____ is a sub-discipline and type of marketing. There are two main definitional characteristics which distinguish it from other types of marketing. The first is that it attempts to send its messages directly to consumers, without the use of intervening media.

a. Power III
b. Direct Marketing Associations
c. Database marketing
d. Direct marketing

14. _____ is defined by the American _____ Association as the activity, set of institutions, and processes for creating, communicating, delivering, and exchanging offerings that have value for customers, clients, partners, and society at large. The term developed from the original meaning which referred literally to going to market, as in shopping, or going to a market to sell goods or services.

_____ practice tends to be seen as a creative industry, which includes advertising, distribution and selling.

a. Gatefold
b. Product naming
c. Business marketing
d. Marketing

15. _____ are national trade organizations that seek to advance all forms of direct marketing.

23 direct marketing trade associations from five continents established an International Federation of _____. Founded in 1989, the IFDirect Marketing Associations was established to develop firm lines of communications between direct marketers around the world, and is dedicated to improving the practice and communicating the value of direct marketing; and to promoting the highest standards for ethical conduct and effective self-regulation of the direct marketing community.

a. Database marketing
b. Power III
c. Direct marketing
d. Direct Marketing Associations

16. A _____ is a structured collection of records or data that is stored in a computer system. The structure is achieved by organizing the data according to a _____ model. The model in most common use today is the relational model.

a. 6-3-5 Brainwriting
b. 180SearchAssistant
c. Power III
d. Database

## Chapter 13. Communicating Customer Value: Personal Selling and Direct Marketing

17. The _____ is an independent agency of the United States government, established in 1914 by the _____ Act. Its principal mission is the promotion of 'consumer protection' and the elimination and prevention of what regulators perceive to be harmfully 'anti-competitive' business practices, such as coercive monopoly.

The _____ Act was one of President Wilson's major acts against trusts.

a. Power III
b. Federal Trade Commission
c. 6-3-5 Brainwriting
d. 180SearchAssistant

18. _____ are long-format television commercials, typically five minutes or longer.. _____ are also known as paid programming (or teleshopping in Europe.) Originally, they were a phenomenon that started in the United States where they were typically shown overnight (usually 2:00 a.m. to 6:00 a.m.)

a. AMAX
b. Infomercials
c. ADTECH
d. ACNielsen

19. _____ consists of the sale of goods or merchandise from a fixed location, such as a department store or kiosk in small or individual lots for direct consumption by the purchaser. _____ may include subordinated services, such as delivery. Purchasers may be individuals or businesses.

a. Retailing
b. Warehouse club
c. General line of merchandise
d. Scrapstore

20. _____ commonly refers to the electronic retailing / _____ channels industry, which includes such billion dollar companies as Home shoppingN, QVC, eBay, ShopNBC, Buy.com, and Amazon.com. _____ allows consumers to shop for goods while in the privacy of their own home, as opposed to traditional shopping, which requires you to visit brick and mortar stores and shopping malls.

The _____ / electronic retailing industry was created in 1977 when small market radio talk show host Bob Circosta was asked to sell avocado-green-colored can openers live on the air by station owner Bud Paxson when an advertiser traded 112 units of product instead of paying his advertising bill.

a. Power III
b. 6-3-5 Brainwriting
c. 180SearchAssistant
d. Home Shopping

21. In the Mediterranean Basin and the Near East, a _____ is a small, separated garden pavilion open on some or all sides. _____s were common in Persia, India, Pakistan, and in the Ottoman Empire from the 13th century onward. Today, there are many _____s in and around the Topkapı Palace in Istanbul, and they are still a relatively common sight in Greece.

a. 180SearchAssistant
b. Kiosk
c. 6-3-5 Brainwriting
d. Power III

22. _____ is a super-regional shopping mall located in the Twin Cities suburb of Bloomington, Minnesota. The mall is located southeast of the junction of Interstate 494 and Minnesota State Highway 77, north of the Minnesota River and is across the interstate from the Minneapolis-St. Paul International Airport. In the United States, it is the second largest enclosed mall in terms of retail space but is largest in terms of total enclosed floor area.

## Chapter 13. Communicating Customer Value: Personal Selling and Direct Marketing

a. 180SearchAssistant
b. Power III
c. 6-3-5 Brainwriting
d. Mall of America

23. _____ is the examining of goods or services from retailers with the intent to purchase at that time. _____ is an activity of selection and/or purchase. In some contexts it is considered a leisure activity as well as an economic one.
a. Shopping
b. Discount store
c. Hawkers
d. Khodebshchik

24. A personal and cultural _____ is a relative ethic _____, an assumption upon which implementation can be extrapolated. A _____ system is a set of consistent _____s and measures that is soo not true. A principle _____ is a foundation upon which other _____s and measures of integrity are based.
a. Dolly Dimples
b. Value
c. Private branding
d. Customization

25. In statistics, _____ has two related meanings:

- the arithmetic _____
- the expected value of a random variable, which is also called the population _____.

It is sometimes stated that the '_____' _____s average. This is incorrect if '_____' is taken in the specific sense of 'arithmetic _____' as there are different types of averages: the _____, median, and mode. For instance, average house prices almost always use the median value for the average. These three types of averages are all measures of locations.

a. Confounding variables
b. Standard score
c. Null hypothesis
d. Mean

26. _____ is a branch of philosophy which seeks to address questions about morality, such as how a moral outcome can be achieved in a specific situation (applied _____), how moral values should be determined (normative _____), what moral values people actually abide by (descriptive _____), what the fundamental semantic, ontological, and epistemic nature of _____ or morality is (meta-_____), and how moral capacity or moral agency develops and what its nature is (moral psychology.)

Socrates was one of the first Greek philosophers to encourage both scholars and the common citizen to turn their attention from the outside world to the condition of man. In this view, Knowledge having a bearing on human life was placed highest, all other knowledge being secondary.

a. ACNielsen
b. ADTECH
c. AMAX
d. Ethics

27. _____ is the area of law concerned with the protection and preservation of the privacy rights of individuals. Increasingly, governments and other public as well as private organizations collect vast amounts of personal information about individuals for a variety of purposes. The law of privacy regulates the type of information which may be collected and how this information may be used.

a. Trademark attorney
b. Privacy law
c. Robinson-Patman Act
d. Covenant not to compete

28. _____s function as professionals who deal with trade, dealing in commodities that they do not produce themselves, in order to produce profit.

_____s can be of two types:

1. A wholesale _____ operates in the chain between producer and retail _____. Some wholesale _____s only organize the movement of goods rather than move the goods themselves.
2. A retail _____ or retailer, sells commodities to consumers (including businesses.) A shop owner is a retail _____.

A _____ class characterizes many pre-modern societies. Its status can range from high (even achieving titles like that of _____ prince or nabob) to low, such as in Chinese culture, due to the soiling capabilities of profiting from 'mere' trade, rather than from the labor of others reflected in agricultural produce, craftsmanship, and tribute.

In the United States, '_____' is defined (under the Uniform Commercial Code) as any person while engaged in a business or profession or a seller who deals regularly in the type of goods sold.

a. Trade credit
b. Countertrade
c. Retail loss prevention
d. Merchant

29. _____ is the ability of an individual or group to seclude themselves or information about themselves and thereby reveal themselves selectively. The boundaries and content of what is considered private differ among cultures and individuals, but share basic common themes. _____ is sometimes related to anonymity, the wish to remain unnoticed or unidentified in the public realm.

a. 6-3-5 Brainwriting
b. 180SearchAssistant
c. Power III
d. Privacy

## Chapter 14. Marketing In the Digital Age

1. The _____ is an economic indicator that measures the satisfaction of consumers across the U.S. economy. It is produced by the National Quality Research Center (NQRC) at the University of Michigan in Ann Arbor, Michigan.

The _____ interviews about 80,000 Americans annually and asks about their satisfaction with the goods and services they have consumed.

   a. American Customer Satisfaction Index
   b. AMAX
   c. ADTECH
   d. ACNielsen

2. _____, a business term, is a measure of how products and services supplied by a company meet or surpass customer expectation. It is seen as a key performance indicator within business and is part of the four perspectives of a Balanced Scorecard.

In a competitive marketplace where businesses compete for customers, _____ is seen as a key differentiator and increasingly has become a key element of business strategy.

   a. Customer Satisfaction
   b. Safety stock
   c. Psychological pricing
   d. Street date

3. An _____ is a private network that uses Internet protocols, network connectivity, and possibly the public telecommunication system to securely share part of an organization's information or operations with suppliers, vendors, partners, customers or other businesses. An _____ can be viewed as part of a company's intranet that is extended to users outside the company (e.g.: normally over the Internet.) It has also been described as a 'state of mind' in which the Internet is perceived as a way to do business with a preapproved set of other companies business-to-business (B2B), in isolation from all other Internet users.

   a. ADTECH
   b. AMAX
   c. ACNielsen
   d. Extranet

4. _____ is defined by the American _____ Association as the activity, set of institutions, and processes for creating, communicating, delivering, and exchanging offerings that have value for customers, clients, partners, and society at large. The term developed from the original meaning which referred literally to going to market, as in shopping, or going to a market to sell goods or services.

_____ practice tends to be seen as a creative industry, which includes advertising, distribution and selling.

   a. Marketing
   b. Business marketing
   c. Product naming
   d. Gatefold

5. A _____ is a process that can allow an organization to concentrate its limited resources on the greatest opportunities to increase sales and achieve a sustainable competitive advantage. A _____ should be centered around the key concept that customer satisfaction is the main goal.

A _____ is most effective when it is an integral component of corporate strategy, defining how the organization will successfully engage customers, prospects, and competitors in the market arena.

a. Law of disruption
b. Vertical market
c. Marketspace
d. Marketing strategy

6. _____, also referred to as i-marketing, web marketing, online marketing is the marketing of products or services over the Internet.

The Internet has brought many unique benefits to marketing, one of which being lower costs for the distribution of information and media to a global audience. The interactive nature of _____, both in terms of providing instant response and eliciting responses, is a unique quality of the medium.

a. ACNielsen
b. ADTECH
c. AMAX
d. Internet marketing

7. A _____ is a plan of action designed to achieve a particular goal.

_____ is different from tactics. In military terms, tactics is concerned with the conduct of an engagement while _____ is concerned with how different engagements are linked.

a. Power III
b. 6-3-5 Brainwriting
c. 180SearchAssistant
d. Strategy

8. _____ is a broad label that refers to any individuals or households that use goods and services generated within the economy. The concept of a _____ is used in different contexts, so that the usage and significance of the term may vary.

A _____ is a person who uses any product or service.

a. Power III
b. 6-3-5 Brainwriting
c. 180SearchAssistant
d. Consumer

9. Electronic commerce, commonly known as _____ or eCommerce, consists of the buying and selling of products or services over electronic systems such as the Internet and other computer networks. The amount of trade conducted electronically has grown extraordinarily with wide-spread Internet usage. A wide variety of commerce is conducted in this way, spurring and drawing on innovations in electronic funds transfer, supply chain management, Internet marketing, online transaction processing, electronic data interchange (EDI), inventory management systems, and automated data collection systems.

a. ADTECH
b. ACNielsen
c. AMAX
d. E-commerce

10. _____ - an information and communication based electronic exchange environment - is a relatively new concept in marketing. Since physical boundaries no longer interfere with buy/sell decisions, the world has grown into several industry specific _____s which are integration of marketplaces through sophisticated computer and telecommunication technologies. The term _____ was introduced by Rayport and Sviokla in 1994 (see Rayport, Jeffrey F.

a. Vertical market
b. Marketspace
c. Blitz QFD
d. Brand infiltration

11. Procter is a surname, and may also refer to:

- Bryan Waller Procter (pseud. Barry Cornwall), English poet
- Goodwin Procter, American law firm
- _____, consumer products multinational

a. Comparison-Shopping agent  
c. Developed country  
b. Push  
d. Procter ' Gamble

12. _____ is a term commonly used to describe commerce transactions between businesses like the one between a manufacturer and a wholesaler or a wholesaler and a retailer i.e both the buyer and the seller are business entity.This is unlike business-to-consumers (B2C) which involve a business entity and end consumer, or business-to-government (B2G) which involve a business entity and government.

The volume of B2B transactions is much higher than the volume of B2C transactions. The primary reason for this is that in a typical supply chain there will be many B2B transactions involving subcomponent or raw materials, and only one B2C transaction, specifically sale of the finished product to the end customer.

a. Disruptive technology  
c. Customer analytics  
b. Cannibalization  
d. Business-to-business

13. A _____ is a type of website, usually maintained by an individual with regular entries of commentary, descriptions of events, or other material such as graphics or video. Entries are commonly displayed in reverse-chronological order. '_____' can also be used as a verb, meaning to maintain or add content to a _____.

a. 6-3-5 Brainwriting  
c. Power III  
b. 180SearchAssistant  
d. Blog

14. _____ is an electronic commerce business model in which consumers (individuals) offer products and services to companies and the companies pay them. This business model is a complete reversal of traditional business model where companies offer goods and services to consumers (business-to-consumer = B2C.)

This kind of economic relationship is qualified as an inverted business model.

a. Trade name  
c. Commodity chain  
b. Total benefits of ownership  
d. Consumer-to-business

15. _____ in economics and business is the result of an exchange and from that trade we assign a numerical monetary value to a good, service or asset. If I trade 4 apples for an orange, the _____ of an orange is 4 - apples. Inversely, the _____ of an apple is 1/4 oranges.

a. Transfer pricing  
c. Price war  
b. Contribution margin-based pricing  
d. Price

16. _____ is the examining of goods or services from retailers with the intent to purchase at that time. _____ is an activity of selection and/or purchase. In some contexts it is considered a leisure activity as well as an economic one.

## Chapter 14. Marketing In the Digital Age

a. Hawkers
c. Discount store
b. Khodebshchik
d. Shopping

17. _____ is an advertisement in which a particular product specifically mentions a competitor by name for the express purpose of showing why the competitor is inferior to the product naming it.

This should not be confused with parody advertisements, where a fictional product is being advertised for the purpose of poking fun at the particular advertisement, nor should it be confused with the use of a coined brand name for the purpose of comparing the product without actually naming an actual competitor. ('Wikipedia tastes better and is less filling than the Encyclopedia Galactica.')

In the 1980s, during what has been referred to as the cola wars, soft-drink manufacturer Pepsi ran a series of advertisements where people, caught on hidden camera, in a blind taste test, chose Pepsi over rival Coca-Cola.

a. Cost per conversion
c. Heavy-up
b. GL-70
d. Comparative advertising

18. A _____ is an entity that provides services to other entities. Usually this refers to a business that provides subscription or web service to other businesses or individuals. Examples of these services include Internet access, Mobile phone operator, and web application hosting.
a. Service provider
c. Multi-level marketing
b. Cross-selling
d. Pay to surf

19. _____ is a form of communication that typically attempts to persuade potential customers to purchase or to consume more of a particular brand of product or service. 'While now central to the contemporary global economy and the reproduction of global production networks, it is only quite recently that _____ has been more than a marginal influence on patterns of sales and production. The formation of modern _____ was intimately bound up with the emergence of new forms of monopoly capitalism around the end of the 19th and beginning of the 20th century as one element in corporate strategies to create, organize and where possible control markets, especially for mass produced consumer goods.
a. ADTECH
c. ACNielsen
b. AMAX
d. Advertising

20. A _____ or banner ad is a form of advertising on the World Wide Web. This form of online advertising entails embedding an advertisement into a web page. It is intended to attract traffic to a website by linking to the website of the advertiser.
a. Spam Lit
c. Web banner
b. Permission marketing
d. Live banner

21. _____ is a form of targeted advertising for advertisements appearing on websites or other media, such as content displayed in mobile browsers. The advertisements themselves are selected and served by automated systems based on the content displayed to the user.

A _____ system scans the text of a website for keywords and returns advertisements to the webpage based on what the user is viewing.

| | |
|---|---|
| a. Contextual advertising | b. Social media optimization |
| c. Cost per action | d. Web analytics |

22. On the World Wide Web, _____s are web pages that are displayed before an expected content page, often to display advertisements or confirm the user's age.

Some people take issue with this form of online advertising. Less controversial uses of _____ pages include introducing another page or site before directing the user to proceed; or alerting the user that the next page requires a login, or has some other requirement which the user should know about before proceeding.

| | |
|---|---|
| a. ADTECH | b. AMAX |
| c. ACNielsen | d. Interstitial |

23. _____ is a form of promotion that uses the Internet and World Wide Web for the expressed purpose of delivering marketing messages to attract customers. Examples of _____ include contextual ads on search engine results pages, banner ads, Rich Media Ads, Social network advertising, online classified advertising, advertising networks and e-mail marketing, including e-mail spam.

Online video directories for brands are a good example of interactive advertising.

| | |
|---|---|
| a. ADTECH | b. AMAX |
| c. Online advertising | d. ACNielsen |

24. _____ are a form of online advertising on the World Wide Web intended to attract web traffic or capture email addresses. It works when certain web sites open a new web browser window to display advertisements. The pop-up window containing an advertisement is usually generated by JavaScript, but can be generated by other means as well.

| | |
|---|---|
| a. Customer intelligence | b. Pop-up ads |
| c. Project Portfolio Management | d. Power III |

25. _____, sometimes referred to as information richness theory, is a framework that can be used to describe a communications medium by describing its ability to reproduce the information sent over it. It was developed by Richard L. Daft and Robert H. Lengel. For example, a phone call will not be able to reproduce visual social cues such as gestures.

| | |
|---|---|
| a. Power III | b. 180SearchAssistant |
| c. 6-3-5 Brainwriting | d. Media richness theory |

26. _____ generally refers to a list of all planned expenses and revenues. It is a plan for saving and spending. A _____ is an important concept in microeconomics, which uses a _____ line to illustrate the trade-offs between two or more goods.

| | |
|---|---|
| a. 6-3-5 Brainwriting | b. Budget |
| c. Power III | d. 180SearchAssistant |

27. _____ is Google's flagship advertising product and main source of revenue ($21 billion in 2008.) _____ offers pay-per-click (PPC) advertising, and site-targeted advertising for both text and banner ads. The _____ program includes local, national, and international distribution.

## Chapter 14. Marketing In the Digital Age

a. AMAX
b. ACNielsen
c. ADTECH
d. AdWords

28. _____ and viral advertising refer to marketing techniques that use pre-existing social networks to produce increases in brand awareness or to achieve other marketing objectives (such as product sales) through self-replicating viral processes, analogous to the spread of pathological and computer viruses. It can be word-of-mouth delivered or enhanced by the network effects of the Internet. Viral promotions may take the form of video clips, interactive Flash games, advergames, ebooks, brandable software, images, or even text messages.

a. Power III
b. New Media Marketing
c. Viral marketing
d. 180SearchAssistant

29. _____ uses online or offline interactive media to communicate with consumers and to promote products, brands, services, and public service announcements, corporate or political groups.

In the inaugural issue of the Journal of _____ , editors Li and Leckenby (2000) defined _____ as the 'paid and unpaid presentation and promotion of products, services and ideas by an identified sponsor through mediated means involving mutual action between consumers and producers.' This is most commonly performed through the Internet as a medium.

It is these mutual actions or interactions that enhance what _____ is trying to achieve.

a. Internet currency
b. Audience Screening
c. Interactive Advertising
d. Enterprise Search Marketing

30. _____ refer to a collection of facts usually collected as the result of experience, observation or experiment or a set of premises. This may consist of numbers, words particularly as measurements or observations of a set of variables. _____ are often viewed as a lowest level of abstraction from which information and knowledge are derived.

a. Randomization
b. P-Value
c. Data
d. Median

31. The _____ is an English-language international daily newspaper published by Dow Jones ' Company in New York City with Asian and European editions. As of 2007, It has a worldwide daily circulation of more than 2 million, with approximately 931,000 paying online subscribers. It was the largest-circulation newspaper in the United States until November 2003, when it was surpassed by USA Today.

a. Power III
b. 180SearchAssistant
c. 6-3-5 Brainwriting
d. Wall Street Journal

32. The _____ is an independent agency of the United States government, established in 1914 by the _____ Act. Its principal mission is the promotion of 'consumer protection' and the elimination and prevention of what regulators perceive to be harmfully 'anti-competitive' business practices, such as coercive monopoly.

The _____ Act was one of President Wilson's major acts against trusts.

a. 6-3-5 Brainwriting
b. Federal Trade Commission
c. Power III
d. 180SearchAssistant

## Chapter 14. Marketing In the Digital Age

33. _____ is the ability of an individual or group to seclude themselves or information about themselves and thereby reveal themselves selectively. The boundaries and content of what is considered private differ among cultures and individuals, but share basic common themes. _____ is sometimes related to anonymity, the wish to remain unnoticed or unidentified in the public realm.
   a. Power III
   b. 6-3-5 Brainwriting
   c. 180SearchAssistant
   d. Privacy

34. _____ is an independent, privately held organization best known for its Web Privacy Seal. _____ runs the world's largest privacy seal program, with more than 2,000 Web sites certified, including the major internet portals and leading brands such as IBM, Oracle Corporation, Intuit and eBay. _____ states its purpose is to establish trusting relationships between individuals and online organizations based on respect for personal identity and information in the evolving networked world.
   a. TRUSTe
   b. 6-3-5 Brainwriting
   c. Power III
   d. 180SearchAssistant

35. _____ is a branch of philosophy which seeks to address questions about morality, such as how a moral outcome can be achieved in a specific situation (applied _____), how moral values should be determined (normative _____), what moral values people actually abide by (descriptive _____), what the fundamental semantic, ontological, and epistemic nature of _____ or morality is (meta-_____), and how moral capacity or moral agency develops and what its nature is (moral psychology.)

Socrates was one of the first Greek philosophers to encourage both scholars and the common citizen to turn their attention from the outside world to the condition of man. In this view, Knowledge having a bearing on human life was placed highest, all other knowledge being secondary.

   a. AMAX
   b. ADTECH
   c. Ethics
   d. ACNielsen

36. The term _____ refers to the gap between people with effective access to digital and information technology and those with very limited or no access at all. It includes the imbalances in physical access to technology as well as the imbalances in resources and skills needed to effectively participate as a digital citizen. In other words, it is the unequal access by some members of society to information and communication technology, and the unequal acquisition of related skills.
   a. Digital divide
   b. 6-3-5 Brainwriting
   c. 180SearchAssistant
   d. Power III

37. _____ is a crime used to refer to fraud that involves someone pretending to be someone else in order to steal money or get other benefits. The term is relatively new and is actually a misnomer, since it is not inherently possible to steal an identity, only to use it. The person whose identity is used can suffer various consequences when he or she is held responsible for the perpetrator's actions.
   a. AMAX
   b. ADTECH
   c. ACNielsen
   d. Identity Theft

38. In the field of computer security, _____ is the criminally fraudulent process of attempting to acquire sensitive information such as usernames, passwords and credit card details by masquerading as a trustworthy entity in an electronic communication. Communications purporting to be from popular social web sites, auction sites, online payment processors or IT Administrators are commonly used to lure the unsuspecting public. _____ is typically carried out by e-mail or instant messaging, and it often directs users to enter details at a fake website whose look and feel are almost identical to the legitimate one.
   a. Telemarketing
   b. Joe job
   c. Phishing
   d. Directory Harvest Attack

## Chapter 15. The Global Marketplace

1. The Oxford University Press defines _____ as 'marketing on a worldwide scale reconciling or taking commercial advantage of global operational differences, similarities and opportunities in order to meet global objectives.' Oxford University Press' Glossary of Marketing Terms.

Here are three reasons for the shift from domestic to _____ as given by the authors of the textbook, _____ Management--3rd Edition by Masaaki Kotabe and Kristiaan Helsen, 2004.

One of the product categories in which global competition has been easy to track is in U.S. automotive sales.

   a. Relationship marketing
   b. Global marketing
   c. Cause-related Marketing
   d. Guerrilla Marketing

2. The _____ or gross domestic income (GDI) is one of the measures of national income and output for a given country's economy. It is the total value of all final goods and services produced in a particular economy; the dollar value of all goods and services produced within a country's borders in a given year. _____ can be defined in three ways, all of which are conceptually identical.
   a. Gross domestic product
   b. Law of demand
   c. Perfect competition
   d. Money

3. _____ is a form of communication that typically attempts to persuade potential customers to purchase or to consume more of a particular brand of product or service. 'While now central to the contemporary global economy and the reproduction of global production networks, it is only quite recently that _____ has been more than a marginal influence on patterns of sales and production. The formation of modern _____ was intimately bound up with the emergence of new forms of monopoly capitalism around the end of the 19th and beginning of the 20th century as one element in corporate strategies to create, organize and where possible control markets, especially for mass produced consumer goods.
   a. AMAX
   b. ADTECH
   c. ACNielsen
   d. Advertising

4. _____ is defined by the American _____ Association as the activity, set of institutions, and processes for creating, communicating, delivering, and exchanging offerings that have value for customers, clients, partners, and society at large. The term developed from the original meaning which referred literally to going to market, as in shopping, or going to a market to sell goods or services.

_____ practice tends to be seen as a creative industry, which includes advertising, distribution and selling.

   a. Gatefold
   b. Business marketing
   c. Marketing
   d. Product naming

5. The _____ is an international organization designed to supervise and liberalize international trade. The _____ came into being on 1 January 1995, and is the successor to the General Agreement on Tariffs and Trade (GATT), which was created in 1947, and continued to operate for almost five decades as a de facto international organization.

The _____ deals with the rules of trade between nations at a near-global level; it is responsible for negotiating and implementing new trade agreements, and is in charge of policing member countries' adherence to all the _____ agreements, signed by the majority of the world's trading nations and ratified in their parliaments.

## Chapter 15. The Global Marketplace 115

a. Merchandise Mart
b. World Trade Organization
c. BSI Group
d. John F. Kennedy International Airport

6. _____ is a measure of the strength of a brand, product, service relative to competitive offerings. There is often a geographic element to the competitive landscape. In defining _____, you must see to what extent a product, brand, or firm controls a product category in a given geographic area.
a. Discretionary spending
b. Market system
c. Market dominance
d. Productivity

7. _____ is exchange of capital, goods, and services across international borders or territories. In most countries, it represents a significant share of gross domestic product (GDP.) While _____ has been present throughout much of history, its economic, social, and political importance has been on the rise in recent centuries.
a. ACNielsen
b. Incoterms
c. ADTECH
d. International trade

8. _____s is the social science that studies the production, distribution, and consumption of goods and services. The term _____s comes from the Ancient Greek οἰκονομία from οἶκος (oikos, 'house') + νόμος (nomos, 'custom' or 'law'), hence 'rules of the house(hold)'. Current _____ models developed out of the broader field of political economy in the late 19th century, owing to a desire to use an empirical approach more akin to the physical sciences.
a. Industrial organization
b. ACNielsen
c. ADTECH
d. Economic

9. The _____ is an economic and political union of 27 member states, located primarily in Europe. It was established by the Treaty of Maastricht on 1 November 1993 upon the foundations of the pre-existing European Economic Community. With almost 500 million citizens, the _____ combined generates an estimated 30% share (US$16.8 trillion in 2007) of the nominal gross world product.
a. Eurozone
b. ADTECH
c. ACNielsen
d. European Union

10. A _____ or export processing zone (EPZ) is one or more special areas of a country where some normal trade barriers such as tariffs and quotas are eliminated and bureaucratic requirements are lowered in hopes of attracting new business and foreign investments. It is a a region where a group of countries has agreed to reduce or eliminate trade barriers. They can be defined as labor intensive manufacturing centers that involve the import of raw materials or components and the export of factory products.
a. Customs union
b. Free trade zone
c. Competitive
d. Green market

11. The _____ was the outcome of the failure of negotiating governments to create the International Trade Organization (ITO.) GATT was formed in 1947 and lasted until 1994, when it was replaced by the World Trade Organization. The Bretton Woods Conference had introduced the idea for an organization to regulate trade as part of a larger plan for economic recovery after World War II.
a. Trade pact
b. General Agreement on Trade in Services
c. Power III
d. General Agreement on Tariffs and Trade

12. A _____ is a tax imposed on goods when they are moved across a political boundary. They are usually associated with protectionism, the economic policy of restraining trade between nations. For political reasons, _____s are usually imposed on imported goods, although they may also be imposed on exported goods.
   a. Power III
   b. Fiscal policy
   c. Tariff
   d. Monetary policy

13. _____ is a designated group of countries that have agreed to eliminate tariffs, quotas and preferences on most (if not all) goods and services traded between them. It can be considered the second stage of economic integration. Countries choose this kind of economic integration form if their economical structures are complementary.
   a. 180SearchAssistant
   b. Free Trade Area
   c. Power III
   d. 6-3-5 Brainwriting

14. The _____ is a trilateral trade bloc in North America created by the governments of the United States, Canada, and Mexico. It superseded the Canada-United States Free Trade Agreement between the US and Canada.

Following diplomatic negotiations dating back to 1990 between the three nations, the leaders met in San Antonio, Texas on December 17, 1992 to sign _____.

   a. 6-3-5 Brainwriting
   b. Power III
   c. 180SearchAssistant
   d. North American Free Trade Agreement

15. In economics, _____ is how a nation's total economy is distributed among its population. . _____ has always been a central concern of economic theory and economic policy. Classical economists such as Adam Smith, Thomas Malthus and David Ricardo were mainly concerned with factor _____, that is, the distribution of income between the main factors of production, land, labour and capital.
   a. Inflation rate
   b. Income distribution
   c. Internality
   d. ACNielsen

16. The _____ is an international financial institution that provides financial and technical assistance to developing countries for development programs (e.g. bridges, roads, schools, etc.) with the stated goal of reducing poverty.

The _____ differs from the _____ Group, in that the _____ comprises only two institutions:

- International Bank for Reconstruction and Development (IBRD)
- International Development Association (IDA)

Whereas the latter incorporates these two in addition to three more:

- International Finance Corporation (IFC)
- Multilateral Investment Guarantee Agency (MIGA)
- International Centre for Settlement of Investment Disputes (ICSID)

John Maynard Keynes (right) represented the UK at the conference, and Harry Dexter White represented the US.

The _____ was created following the ratification of the United Nations Monetary and Financial Conference of the Bretton Woods agreement. The concept was originally conceived in July 1944 at the United Nations Monetary and Financial Conference.

a. World Bank
b. 6-3-5 Brainwriting
c. Power III
d. 180SearchAssistant

17. _____ is one of the four elements of marketing mix. An organization or set of organizations (go-betweens) involved in the process of making a product or service available for use or consumption by a consumer or business user.

The other three parts of the marketing mix are product, pricing, and promotion.

a. Clustering
b. LIFO
c. Better Living Through Chemistry
d. Distribution

18. _____ is a type of trade in which goods or services are directly exchanged for other goods and/or services, without the use of money. It can be bilateral or multilateral, and usually exists parallel to monetary systems in most developed countries, though to a very limited extent. _____ usually replaces money as the method of exchange in times of monetary crisis, when the currency is unstable and devalued by hyperinflation.

a. Black market
b. Protectionism
c. Mixed economy
d. Barter

19. _____ is exchanging goods or services that are paid for, in whole or part, with other goods or services.

There are five main variants of _____:

- Barter: Exchange of goods or services directly for other goods or services without the use of money as means of purchase or payment.
- Switch trading: Practice in which one company sells to another its obligation to make a purchase in a given country.
- Counter purchase: Sale of goods and services to a country by a company that promises to make a future purchase of a specific product from the country.
- Buyback: occurs when a firm builds a plant in a country - or supplies technology, equipment, training, or other services to the country and agrees to take a certain percentage of the plant's output as partial payment for the contract.
- Offset: Agreement that a company will offset a hard - currency purchase of an unspecified product from that nation in the future. Agreement by one nation to buy a product from another, subject to the purchase of some or all of the components and raw materials from the buyer of the finished product, or the assembly of such product in the buyer nation.

a. Retail loss prevention
b. RFM
c. Merchant
d. Countertrade

## Chapter 15. The Global Marketplace

20. A _____ is the space, actual or metaphorical, in which a market operates. The term is also used in a trademark law context to denote the actual consumer environment, ie. the 'real world' in which products and services are provided and consumed.
    a. 6-3-5 Brainwriting
    b. 180SearchAssistant
    c. Power III
    d. Marketplace

21. _____ is the term used for the influence the United States of America has on the culture of other countries, resulting in such phenomena as the substitution of a given culture with American culture. When encountered unwillingly or perforce, it usually has a negative connotation; when sought voluntarily, it sometimes has a positive connotation. Before the mid-twentieth century, however, _____ referred to the process by which immigrants to the United States became American.
    a. AMAX
    b. ACNielsen
    c. ADTECH
    d. Americanization

22. _____ in its literal sense is the process of transformation of local or regional phenomena into global ones. It can be described as a process by which the people of the world are unified into a single society and function together.

    This process is a combination of economic, technological, sociocultural and political forces.

    a. Power III
    b. 180SearchAssistant
    c. 6-3-5 Brainwriting
    d. Globalization

23. Procter is a surname, and may also refer to:
    - Bryan Waller Procter (pseud. Barry Cornwall), English poet
    - Goodwin Procter, American law firm
    - _____, consumer products multinational

    a. Push
    b. Comparison-Shopping agent
    c. Developed country
    d. Procter ' Gamble

24. A _____ is a firm that manufactures components or products for another 'hiring' firm. Many industries utilize this process, especially the aerospace, defense, computer, semiconductor, energy, medical, food manufacturing, personal care, and automotive fields. Some types of contract manufacturing include CNC machining, complex assembly, aluminum die casting, grinding, broaching, gears, and forging.
    a. Power III
    b. 180SearchAssistant
    c. Productivity
    d. Contract manufacturer

25. The verb _____ or grant _____ means to give permission. The noun _____ refers to that permission as well as to the document memorializing that permission. _____ may be granted by a party to another party as an element of an agreement between those parties.
    a. License
    b. Power III
    c. 180SearchAssistant
    d. 6-3-5 Brainwriting

## Chapter 15. The Global Marketplace

26. _____ is the state or fact of exclusive rights and control over property, which may be an object, land/real estate, or some other kind of property (like government-granted monopolies collectively referred to as intellectual property.) It is embodied in an _____ right also referred to as title.

_____ is the key building block in the development of the capitalist socio-economic system.

a. ADTECH
b. AMAX
c. ACNielsen
d. Ownership

27. Foreign _____ in its classic form is defined as a company from one country making a physical investment into building a factory in another country. It is the establishment of an enterprise by a foreigner. Its definition can be extended to include investments made to acquire lasting interest in enterprises operating outside of the economy of the investor.

a. Green Earth Market
b. Direct investment
c. Westinghouse Electric
d. Capital Cities/ABC

28. A _____ is a collection of symbols, experiences and associations connected with a product, a service, a person or any other artifact or entity.

_____s have become increasingly important components of culture and the economy, now being described as 'cultural accessories and personal philosophies'.

Some people distinguish the psychological aspect of a _____ from the experiential aspect.

a. Naming rights
b. Brand
c. Status brand
d. Lovemarks

29. The _____ is generally accepted as the use and specification of the four p's describing the strategic position of a product in the marketplace. One version of the origins of the _____ starts in 1948 when James Culliton said that a marketing decision should be a result of something similar to a recipe. This version continued in 1953 when Neil Borden, in his American Marketing Association presidential address, took the recipe idea one step further and coined the term 'Marketing-Mix'.

a. 6-3-5 Brainwriting
b. 180SearchAssistant
c. Power III
d. Marketing mix

30. _____s are versions of the same parent product that serve a segment of the target market and increase the variety of an offering. An example of a _____ is Coke vs. Diet Coke in same product category of soft drinks. This tactic is undertaken due to the brand loyalty and brand awareness they enjoy consumers are more likely to buy a new product that has a tried and trusted brand name on it.

a. Brand culture
b. Product extension
c. Retail design
d. Corporate identity

## Chapter 15. The Global Marketplace

31. _____ involves disseminating information about a product, product line, brand, or company. It is one of the four key aspects of the marketing mix. (The other three elements are product marketing, pricing, and distribution). P>_____ is generally sub-divided into two parts:

- Above the line _____: Promotion in the media (e.g. TV, radio, newspapers, Internet and Mobile Phones) in which the advertiser pays an advertising agency to place the ad
- Below the line _____: All other _____. Much of this is intended to be subtle enough for the consumer to be unaware that _____ is taking place. E.g. sponsorship, product placement, endorsements, sales _____, merchandising, direct mail, personal selling, public relations, trade shows

   a. Promotion  
   c. M80  
   b. Technology maturity lifecycle  
   d. Cash and carry

32. _____ in economics and business is the result of an exchange and from that trade we assign a numerical monetary value to a good, service or asset. If I trade 4 apples for an orange, the _____ of an orange is 4 - apples. Inversely, the _____ of an apple is 1/4 oranges.

   a. Contribution margin-based pricing  
   c. Price war  
   b. Transfer pricing  
   d. Price

33. In economics, '_____' can refer to any kind of predatory pricing. However, the word is now generally used only in the context of international trade law, where _____ is defined as the act of a manufacturer in one country exporting a product to another country at a price which is either below the price it charges in its home market or is below its costs of production. The term has a negative connotation, but advocates of free markets see '_____' as beneficial for consumers and believe that protectionism to prevent it would have net negative consequences.

   a. Supreme Court of the United States  
   c. Dumping  
   b. Quantitative  
   d. Brando

34. _____? is an American advertising campaign encouraging the consumption of cow's milk, which was created by the advertising agency Goodby Silverstein ' Partners for the California Milk Processor Board in 1993 and later licensed for use by milk processors and dairy farmers. It has been running since October 1993. The campaign has been credited with greatly increasing milk sales nationwide after a 20-year slump.

   a. For Your Consideration  
   c. You Got the Right One, Baby  
   b. Just Say No  
   d. Got Milk?

35. A high degree of market _____ can result in disintermediation due to the buyer's increased knowledge of supply pricing.

_____ is important since it is one of the theoretical conditions required for a free market to be efficient.

Price _____ can, however, lead to higher prices, if it makes sellers reluctant to give steep discounts to certain buyers, or if it facilitates collusion.

   a. Just-In-Case  
   c. Transparency  
   b. Lobbying and Disclosure Act of 1995  
   d. Clutter

## Chapter 15. The Global Marketplace

36. In economics, an _____ is any good or commodity, transported from one country to another country in a legitimate fashion, typically for use in trade. _____ goods or services are provided to foreign consumers by domestic producers. _____ is an important part of international trade.
   a. AMAX
   b. ADTECH
   c. ACNielsen
   d. Export

37. _____ is the practice of individuals including commercial businesses, governments and institutions, facilitating the sale of their products or services to other companies or organizations that in turn resell them, use them as components in products or services they offer _____ is also called business-to-_____ for short. (Note that while marketing to government entities shares some of the same dynamics of organizational marketing, B2G Marketing is meaningfully different.)
   a. Buy one, get one free
   b. Customer franchise
   c. Marketspace
   d. Business marketing

# Chapter 16. Marketing Ethics and Social Responsibility

1. _____ is a broad label that refers to any individuals or households that use goods and services generated within the economy. The concept of a _____ is used in different contexts, so that the usage and significance of the term may vary.

A _____ is a person who uses any product or service.

 a. Power III
 b. 180SearchAssistant
 c. 6-3-5 Brainwriting
 d. Consumer

2. Electronic commerce, commonly known as _____ or eCommerce, consists of the buying and selling of products or services over electronic systems such as the Internet and other computer networks. The amount of trade conducted electronically has grown extraordinarily with wide-spread Internet usage. A wide variety of commerce is conducted in this way, spurring and drawing on innovations in electronic funds transfer, supply chain management, Internet marketing, online transaction processing, electronic data interchange (EDI), inventory management systems, and automated data collection systems.

 a. ACNielsen
 b. AMAX
 c. ADTECH
 d. E-commerce

3. In economics, business, retail, and accounting, a _____ is the value of money that has been used up to produce something, and hence is not available for use anymore. In economics, a _____ is an alternative that is given up as a result of a decision. In business, the _____ may be one of acquisition, in which case the amount of money expended to acquire it is counted as _____.

 a. Fixed costs
 b. Marginal cost
 c. Transaction cost
 d. Cost

4. _____ is one of the four elements of marketing mix. An organization or set of organizations (go-betweens) involved in the process of making a product or service available for use or consumption by a consumer or business user.

The other three parts of the marketing mix are product, pricing, and promotion.

 a. Distribution
 b. LIFO
 c. Better Living Through Chemistry
 d. Clustering

5. _____ is defined by the American _____ Association as the activity, set of institutions, and processes for creating, communicating, delivering, and exchanging offerings that have value for customers, clients, partners, and society at large. The term developed from the original meaning which referred literally to going to market, as in shopping, or going to a market to sell goods or services.

_____ practice tends to be seen as a creative industry, which includes advertising, distribution and selling.

 a. Gatefold
 b. Business marketing
 c. Product naming
 d. Marketing

6. _____ in economics and business is the result of an exchange and from that trade we assign a numerical monetary value to a good, service or asset. If I trade 4 apples for an orange, the _____ of an orange is 4 - apples. Inversely, the _____ of an apple is 1/4 oranges.

a. Price  
b. Transfer pricing  
c. Price war  
d. Contribution margin-based pricing

7. _____ is a form of communication that typically attempts to persuade potential customers to purchase or to consume more of a particular brand of product or service. 'While now central to the contemporary global economy and the reproduction of global production networks, it is only quite recently that _____ has been more than a marginal influence on patterns of sales and production. The formation of modern _____ was intimately bound up with the emergence of new forms of monopoly capitalism around the end of the 19th and beginning of the 20th century as one element in corporate strategies to create, organize and where possible control markets, especially for mass produced consumer goods.
a. ACNielsen  
b. Advertising  
c. AMAX  
d. ADTECH

8. _____ involves disseminating information about a product, product line, brand, or company. It is one of the four key aspects of the marketing mix. (The other three elements are product marketing, pricing, and distribution). P>_____ is generally sub-divided into two parts:

- Above the line _____: Promotion in the media (e.g. TV, radio, newspapers, Internet and Mobile Phones) in which the advertiser pays an advertising agency to place the ad
- Below the line _____: All other _____. Much of this is intended to be subtle enough for the consumer to be unaware that _____ is taking place. E.g. sponsorship, product placement, endorsements, sales _____, merchandising, direct mail, personal selling, public relations, trade shows

a. M80  
b. Technology maturity lifecycle  
c. Cash and carry  
d. Promotion

9. _____ as a legal term refers to promotional statements and claims that express subjective rather than objective views, such that no reasonable person would take literally. _____ is especially featured in testimonials.

In a legal context, the term originated in the English Court of Appeal case Carlill v Carbolic Smoke Ball Company, which centred on whether a monetary reimbursement should be paid when an influenza preventative device failed to work.

a. Heinz pickle pin  
b. Conquesting  
c. Custom media  
d. Puffery

10. The _____ of 1938 is a United States federal law that amended the Federal Trade Commission Act to add the clause 'unfair or deceptive acts or practices in commerce are hereby declared unlawful' to the Section 5 prohibition of unfair methods of competition, in order to protect consumers as well as competition.

1938 amendment to the federal trade commission act that authorized the FTC to restrict unfair or deceptive acts; also called the advertising act. Until this amendment was passed, the FTC could only restrict practices that were unfair to competitors.

a. Covenant not to compete  
b. Real property  
c. Federal Trade Commission Act  
d. Wheeler-Lea Act

## Chapter 16. Marketing Ethics and Social Responsibility

11. _____ is one of the four Ps of the marketing mix. The other three aspects are product, promotion, and place. It is also a key variable in microeconomic price allocation theory.
   a. Cost-plus pricing
   b. Transfer pricing
   c. Resale price maintenance
   d. Pricing

12. Procter is a surname, and may also refer to:

   - Bryan Waller Procter (pseud. Barry Cornwall), English poet
   - Goodwin Procter, American law firm
   - _____, consumer products multinational

   a. Developed country
   b. Procter ' Gamble
   c. Push
   d. Comparison-Shopping agent

13. _____ is an American magazine published monthly by Consumers Union. It publishes reviews and comparisons of consumer products and services based on reporting and results from its in-house testing laboratory. It also publishes cleaning and general buying guides.
   a. Magalog
   b. Power III
   c. Consumer Reports
   d. Crossing the Chasm

14. _____ is an independent, nonprofit testing and information organization serving consumers in the United States. Its mission is to test products, inform the public, and protect consumers. Its income is derived from the sale of its magazine Consumer Reports and other services, and from noncommercial contributions, grants, and fees.
   a. Multinational corporation
   b. Green Earth Market
   c. Forrester Research
   d. Consumers Union

15. _____ is the process of a product becoming obsolete and/or non-functional after a certain period or amount of use in a way that is planned or designed by the manufacturer. _____ has potential benefits for a producer because the product fails and the consumer is under pressure to purchase again, whether from the same manufacturer (a replacement part or a newer model), or from a competitor which might also rely on _____. The purpose of _____ is to hide the real cost per use from the consumer, and charge a higher price than they would otherwise be willing to pay (or would be unwilling to spend all at once.)
   a. 180SearchAssistant
   b. 6-3-5 Brainwriting
   c. Power III
   d. Planned obsolescence

16. _____ is an advertisement in which a particular product specifically mentions a competitor by name for the express purpose of showing why the competitor is inferior to the product naming it.

This should not be confused with parody advertisements, where a fictional product is being advertised for the purpose of poking fun at the particular advertisement, nor should it be confused with the use of a coined brand name for the purpose of comparing the product without actually naming an actual competitor. ('Wikipedia tastes better and is less filling than the Encyclopedia Galactica.')

In the 1980s, during what has been referred to as the cola wars, soft-drink manufacturer Pepsi ran a series of advertisements where people, caught on hidden camera, in a blind taste test, chose Pepsi over rival Coca-Cola.

a. Heavy-up  
c. GL-70  
b. Cost per conversion  
d. Comparative advertising

17. The philosophy of _____ holds that the only thing that exists is matter, and is considered a form of physicalism. Fundamentally, all things are composed of material and all phenomena (including consciousness) are the result of material interactions; therefore, matter is the only substance. As a theory, _____ belongs to the class of monist ontology.
   a. Materialism
   c. 6-3-5 Brainwriting
   b. Power III
   d. 180SearchAssistant

18. _____ is the examining of goods or services from retailers with the intent to purchase at that time. _____ is an activity of selection and/or purchase. In some contexts it is considered a leisure activity as well as an economic one.
   a. Discount store
   c. Hawkers
   b. Khodebshchik
   d. Shopping

19. _____ is a rivalry between individuals, groups, nations for territory, a niche, or allocation of resources. It arises whenever two or more parties strive for a goal which cannot be shared. _____ occurs naturally between living organisms which co-exist in the same environment.
   a. Non-price competition
   c. Competition
   b. Direct competition
   d. Price fixing

20. _____ is the practice of selling a product or service at a very low price, intending to drive competitors out of the market, or create barriers to entry for potential new competitors. If competitors or potential competitors cannot sustain equal or lower prices without losing money, they go out of business or choose not to enter the business. The predatory merchant then has fewer competitors or is even a de facto monopoly, and can then raise prices above what the market would otherwise bear.
   a. 180SearchAssistant
   c. Power III
   b. List price
   d. Predatory pricing

21. _____ is the equation of personal happiness with consumption and the purchase of material possessions.

The term is often associated with criticisms of consumption starting with Thorstein Veblen.

Veblen's subject of examination, the newly emergent middle class arising at the turn of the twentieth century, comes to full fruition by the end of the twentieth century through the process of globalization.

In economics, _____ refers to economic policies placing emphasis on consumption.

   a. 6-3-5 Brainwriting
   c. Power III
   b. 180SearchAssistant
   d. Consumerism

22. According to the American Marketing Association, _____ is the marketing of products that are presumed to be environmentally safe. Thus _____ incorporates a broad range of activities, including product modification, changes to the production process, packaging changes, as well as modifying advertising. Yet defining _____ is not a simple task where several meanings intersect and contradict each other; an example of this will be the existence of varying social, environmental and retail definitions attached to this term.

a. Customer analytics
b. Green marketing
c. Perceptual mapping
d. Market segment

23. _____ is a concept whereby environmental protection centers around the product itself, and everyone involved in the lifespan of the product is called upon to take up responsibility to reduce its environmental impact. For manufacturers, this includes planning for, and if necessary, paying for the recycling or disposal of the product at the end of its useful life. This may be achieved, in part, by redesigning products to use fewer harmful substances, to be more durable, reuseable and recycleable, and to make products from recycled materials.

a. Power III
b. Political consumerism
c. SA8000
d. Product stewardship

24. _____ is a global document management company which manufactures and sells a range of color and black-and-white printers, multifunction systems, photo copiers, digital production printing presses, and related consulting services and supplies. Xerox is headquartered in Norwalk, Connecticut , though its largest population of employees is based in and around Rochester, New York, the area in which the company was founded. The Xerox 914 was the first one-piece plain paper photocopier, and sold in the thousands.

Xerox was founded in 1906 in Rochester, New York as 'The Haloid Company', which originally manufactured photographic paper and equipment.

a. Japan Advertising Photographers' Association
b. Green Earth Market
c. Xerox Corporation
d. Partnership for a Drug-Free America

25. The _____ is an economic and political union of 27 member states, located primarily in Europe. It was established by the Treaty of Maastricht on 1 November 1993 upon the foundations of the pre-existing European Economic Community. With almost 500 million citizens, the _____ combined generates an estimated 30% share (US$16.8 trillion in 2007) of the nominal gross world product.

a. ADTECH
b. ACNielsen
c. Eurozone
d. European Union

26. The _____ is a trilateral trade bloc in North America created by the governments of the United States, Canada, and Mexico. It superseded the Canada-United States Free Trade Agreement between the US and Canada.

Following diplomatic negotiations dating back to 1990 between the three nations, the leaders met in San Antonio, Texas on December 17, 1992 to sign _____.

a. Power III
b. North American Free Trade Agreement
c. 6-3-5 Brainwriting
d. 180SearchAssistant

27. _____ refers to 'controlling human or societal behaviour by rules or restrictions.' _____ can take many forms: legal restrictions promulgated by a government authority, self-_____, social _____, co-_____ and market _____. One can consider _____ as actions of conduct imposing sanctions (such as a fine.) This action of administrative law, or implementing regulatory law, may be contrasted with statutory or case law.

a. Robinson-Patman Act
b. Nutrition Labeling and Education Act
c. Consumer protection
d. Regulation

## Chapter 16. Marketing Ethics and Social Responsibility

28. The _____ concept is an enlightened marketing concept that holds that a company should make good marketing decisions by considering consumers' wants, the company's requirements, and society's long-term interests. It is closely linked with the principles of corporate social responsibility and of sustainable development.

The concept has an emphasis on social responsibility and suggests that for a company to only focus on exchange relationship with customers might not be suitable in order to sustain long term success.

a. Societal marketing
b. Customer acquisition management
c. Category management
d. Product differentiation

29. _____ is a branch of philosophy which seeks to address questions about morality, such as how a moral outcome can be achieved in a specific situation (applied _____), how moral values should be determined (normative _____), what moral values people actually abide by (descriptive _____), what the fundamental semantic, ontological, and epistemic nature of _____ or morality is (meta-_____), and how moral capacity or moral agency develops and what its nature is (moral psychology.)

Socrates was one of the first Greek philosophers to encourage both scholars and the common citizen to turn their attention from the outside world to the condition of man. In this view, Knowledge having a bearing on human life was placed highest, all other knowledge being secondary.

a. ADTECH
b. ACNielsen
c. AMAX
d. Ethics

30. _____ is the area of applied ethics which deals with the moral principles behind the operation and regulation of marketing. Some areas of _____ overlap with media ethics.

Possible frameworks:

- Value-oriented framework, analyzing ethical problems on the basis of the values which they infringe (e.g. honesty, autonomy, privacy, transparency.) An example of such an approach is the AMA Statement of Ethics.
- Stakeholder-oriented framework, analysing ethical problems on the basis of whom they affect (e.g. consumers, competitors, society as a whole.)
- Process-oriented framework, analysing ethical problems in terms of the categories used by marketing specialists (e.g. research, price, promotion, placement.)

None of these frameworks allows, by itself, a convenient and complete categorization of the great variety of issues in _____.

Contrary to popular impressions, not all marketing is adversarial, and not all marketing is stacked in favour of the marketer.

a. Power III
b. 180SearchAssistant
c. 6-3-5 Brainwriting
d. Marketing ethics

31. _____ is a sub-discipline and type of marketing. There are two main definitional characteristics which distinguish it from other types of marketing. The first is that it attempts to send its messages directly to consumers, without the use of intervening media.
   a. Power III
   b. Database marketing
   c. Direct Marketing Associations
   d. Direct marketing

32. The _____ is a professional association for marketers. As of 2008 it had approximately 40,000 members. There are collegiate chapters on 250 campuses.
   a. AMAX
   b. American Marketing Association
   c. ACNielsen
   d. ADTECH

# ANSWER KEY

### Chapter 1
| | | | | | | | | | |
|---|---|---|---|---|---|---|---|---|---|
| 1. b | 2. d | 3. b | 4. a | 5. d | 6. d | 7. d | 8. c | 9. b | 10. d |
| 11. b | 12. d | 13. a | 14. c | 15. d | 16. d | 17. d | 18. d | 19. a | 20. d |
| 21. c | 22. d | 23. b | 24. d | 25. d | 26. a | 27. a | 28. c | 29. a | 30. d |
| 31. a | 32. d | 33. d | 34. d | 35. d | 36. c | | | | |

### Chapter 2
| | | | | | | | | | |
|---|---|---|---|---|---|---|---|---|---|
| 1. b | 2. b | 3. a | 4. a | 5. d | 6. d | 7. a | 8. c | 9. d | 10. d |
| 11. d | 12. c | 13. c | 14. c | 15. d | 16. d | 17. c | 18. b | 19. d | 20. c |
| 21. a | 22. a | 23. d | 24. c | 25. b | 26. b | 27. d | 28. d | 29. d | 30. d |
| 31. c | 32. c | 33. b | 34. a | 35. d | 36. a | | | | |

### Chapter 3
| | | | | | | | | | |
|---|---|---|---|---|---|---|---|---|---|
| 1. d | 2. d | 3. d | 4. d | 5. a | 6. d | 7. a | 8. d | 9. b | 10. d |
| 11. d | 12. d | 13. c | 14. d | 15. d | 16. a | 17. c | 18. b | 19. d | 20. d |
| 21. d | 22. a | 23. d | 24. d | 25. d | 26. a | 27. c | 28. d | 29. d | 30. d |
| 31. c | 32. a | 33. d | 34. d | 35. d | 36. b | 37. c | | | |

### Chapter 4
| | | | | | | | | | |
|---|---|---|---|---|---|---|---|---|---|
| 1. c | 2. c | 3. b | 4. c | 5. b | 6. c | 7. d | 8. c | 9. d | 10. d |
| 11. b | 12. d | 13. d | 14. d | 15. d | 16. d | 17. d | 18. a | 19. c | 20. b |
| 21. a | 22. d | 23. d | 24. d | 25. c | 26. d | 27. a | 28. b | 29. d | 30. d |
| 31. b | 32. a | 33. b | 34. d | 35. a | 36. d | 37. c | 38. d | 39. d | 40. c |
| 41. d | 42. d | 43. d | 44. c | 45. d | 46. c | 47. c | 48. d | 49. c | 50. d |
| 51. b | 52. b | 53. b | 54. d | 55. d | 56. a | 57. d | 58. a | 59. d | |

### Chapter 5
| | | | | | | | | | |
|---|---|---|---|---|---|---|---|---|---|
| 1. b | 2. d | 3. d | 4. d | 5. c | 6. d | 7. d | 8. d | 9. a | 10. a |
| 11. d | 12. a | 13. d | 14. d | 15. d | 16. b | 17. c | 18. d | 19. c | 20. c |
| 21. b | 22. d | 23. a | 24. d | 25. d | 26. d | 27. d | 28. d | 29. c | 30. b |
| 31. a | 32. d | 33. d | 34. b | 35. d | 36. a | 37. d | 38. d | 39. c | 40. d |
| 41. c | 42. d | | | | | | | | |

### Chapter 6
| | | | | | | | | | |
|---|---|---|---|---|---|---|---|---|---|
| 1. d | 2. c | 3. d | 4. d | 5. a | 6. d | 7. a | 8. d | 9. b | 10. d |
| 11. b | 12. a | 13. a | 14. d | 15. d | 16. d | 17. c | 18. d | 19. d | 20. d |
| 21. d | 22. d | 23. b | 24. a | 25. a | 26. d | 27. d | 28. d | 29. b | 30. d |
| 31. b | 32. a | 33. a | | | | | | | |

### Chapter 7
| | | | | | | | | | |
|---|---|---|---|---|---|---|---|---|---|
| 1. a | 2. b | 3. d | 4. d | 5. b | 6. a | 7. c | 8. c | 9. b | 10. a |
| 11. d | 12. d | 13. b | 14. d | 15. d | 16. d | 17. d | 18. d | 19. d | 20. b |
| 21. d | 22. a | 23. d | 24. a | 25. d | 26. d | 27. d | 28. c | 29. b | 30. d |
| 31. a | 32. b | 33. d | 34. d | 35. d | 36. b | 37. d | 38. d | 39. c | 40. b |
| 41. c | 42. d | 43. a | 44. b | 45. d | 46. d | 47. a | 48. d | 49. d | 50. d |
| 51. d | | | | | | | | | |

**Chapter 8**
1. c   2. b   3. b   4. b   5. a   6. d   7. b   8. d   9. a   10. d
11. a  12. a  13. a  14. a

**Chapter 9**
1. b   2. d   3. d   4. d   5. d   6. d   7. d   8. d   9. a   10. d
11. d  12. d  13. a  14. b  15. b  16. d  17. c  18. d  19. d  20. d
21. d  22. d  23. d  24. d  25. a  26. d  27. c  28. d  29. d  30. a
31. c  32. b  33. d  34. a  35. d  36. d  37. a  38. b  39. d  40. d
41. d  42. d  43. c  44. d  45. d  46. c  47. c  48. d  49. b  50. a

**Chapter 10**
1. d   2. a   3. a   4. b   5. d   6. c   7. d   8. b   9. d   10. c
11. a  12. a  13. b  14. a  15. a  16. a  17. d  18. a  19. d  20. d
21. d  22. a  23. d  24. a  25. b  26. a  27. d  28. b  29. d  30. a
31. a

**Chapter 11**
1. b   2. b   3. b   4. d   5. a   6. b   7. a   8. b   9. c   10. b
11. d  12. b  13. d  14. d  15. a  16. d  17. d  18. d  19. d  20. b
21. d  22. b  23. a  24. d  25. c  26. a  27. c  28. d  29. a  30. d
31. b  32. b

**Chapter 12**
1. d   2. d   3. d   4. d   5. b   6. d   7. c   8. c   9. c   10. a
11. d  12. a  13. a  14. d  15. d  16. d  17. d  18. b  19. a  20. d
21. c  22. d  23. d  24. c  25. b  26. d  27. b  28. d  29. b  30. d
31. d  32. c  33. d  34. c  35. d  36. d  37. b  38. b  39. d  40. c
41. d  42. d  43. b  44. b  45. b  46. b

**Chapter 13**
1. d   2. c   3. c   4. a   5. a   6. d   7. d   8. d   9. a   10. d
11. d  12. c  13. d  14. d  15. d  16. d  17. b  18. b  19. a  20. d
21. b  22. d  23. a  24. b  25. d  26. d  27. b  28. d  29. d

**Chapter 14**
1. a   2. a   3. d   4. a   5. d   6. d   7. d   8. d   9. d   10. b
11. d  12. d  13. d  14. d  15. d  16. d  17. d  18. a  19. d  20. c
21. a  22. d  23. c  24. b  25. d  26. b  27. d  28. c  29. c  30. c
31. d  32. b  33. d  34. a  35. c  36. a  37. d  38. c

# ANSWER KEY

**Chapter 15**

| 1. b | 2. a | 3. d | 4. c | 5. b | 6. c | 7. d | 8. d | 9. d | 10. b |
| 11. d | 12. c | 13. b | 14. d | 15. b | 16. a | 17. d | 18. d | 19. d | 20. d |
| 21. d | 22. d | 23. d | 24. d | 25. a | 26. d | 27. b | 28. b | 29. d | 30. b |
| 31. a | 32. d | 33. c | 34. d | 35. c | 36. d | 37. d | | | |

**Chapter 16**

| 1. d | 2. d | 3. d | 4. a | 5. d | 6. a | 7. b | 8. d | 9. d | 10. d |
| 11. d | 12. b | 13. c | 14. d | 15. d | 16. d | 17. a | 18. d | 19. c | 20. d |
| 21. d | 22. b | 23. d | 24. c | 25. d | 26. b | 27. d | 28. a | 29. d | 30. d |
| 31. d | 32. b | | | | | | | | |

www.ingramcontent.com/pod-product-compliance
Lightning Source LLC
Chambersburg PA
CBHW082045230426
43670CB00016B/2781